A Lesbian
Love Advisor

Published in the United States by Cleis Press, P.O. Box 8933, Pittsburgh, Pennsylvania 15221, and P.O. Box 14684, San Francisco, California 94114.

Printed in the United States on pH neutral paper.

Typesetting: CalGraphics
Logo art: Juana Alicia
Illustrations: Nicole Ferentz

First Edition.
10 9 8 7 6 5 4

ISBN: 0-939416-27-1 cloth
ISBN: 0-939416-26-3 paper

West, Celeste.
    A lesbian love advisor on the sweet & savory arts of lesbian courtship . . . / by Celeste West ; with the commentaries of Lady Clitoressa & her circle. — 1st ed.
    190 p.   cm.
    Includes index.
    ISBN 0-939416-27-1 : $24.95. — ISBN 0-939416-26-3 (pbk.) : $9.95
    1. Lesbians — Social life and customs.   2. Courtship.   3. Lesbians — sexual behavior.   4. Gidlow, Elsa.   I. West, Celeste, 1942-   II. Title.
    HQ75.5.W47   1989
    306.76'63 — dc20

Grateful acknowledgment is made to the following for permission to reprint previously published material: Booklegger Publishing for "Chains of Fire," from *ELSA, I Come With My Songs: The Autobiography of Elsa Gidlow,* © Elsa Gidlow and Celeste West, 1986, Booklegger Publishing, 555 29th Street, San Francisco 94131; The Buddhist Peace Fellowship for the excerpt from "Rape," © Judith Ragir in *The Path of Compassion,* Parallax Press, 1988; Bernice Johnson Reagon, Songtalk Publishing Co., for chorus from "Every Woman," lyrics and music published in *Compositions One:* © Bernice Johnson Reagon, Box 21350, Washington, D.C. 20009; St. Martin's Press for the journal entry in *Sassafrass, Cypress & Indigo,* © Ntozake Shange, 1982.

A LESBIAN LOVE ADVISOR

A Lesbian Love Advisor *on the sweet & savory arts of Lesbian Courtship, sensualizing them with impeccable Bedside Manners, with sage advice on enjoying* The Divine Lesbian Relationship *in graceful gusto. How to manage* Faux Pas *with Finesse, Jealousy with Mercy and the Apples of Discord without war. Lesbian Rituals, Meta*Physicals, Sorcery & Ceremonies of Life elucidated.*

by

Celeste West

with the commentaries of

Lady Clitoressa & Her Circle

illustrated by

Nicole Ferentz

Cleis Press

For

Sue, Joanne & Elsa,
sine qua non

Dedicated to

Celina,
she stallion of the open meadows.

With Lifelong Hugs

To Cleis Press for countless acts of gallantry;

To Jocelyn Cohen, Peg Cruikshank, Tee Corinne, Joanne Genêt, LaVonne Jacobsen, Carole Leita, and Dorothy Perkins, ladies of penetrating insight and friends who continue to dot my i's with halos;

To the Lesbian Relationship Class of 1988, City College of San Francisco, and Professor Lindy McNight;

To my muses in tails, Bright Eyes, Burma, Concha, Freya and Tara; and,

To Venus Sardonica, whatever form you may come in next.

Contents

About the Author

Celeste West was born a pragmatic romantic in Pocatello, Idaho. She went to finishing school in San Francisco, where she now majors in gracious living with the parade of cats and extended family of a Lesbian-at-large. Besides her calling as a scribe, Celeste manages Booklegger Publishing as well as the library/bookstore of the Zen Center. An occasional carouser, she is every other inch a lady.

Celeste West's books include *Revolting Librarians*, with Elizabeth Katz; *The Passionate Perils of Publishing*, with Valerie Wheat; *Words in Our Pockets: The Feminist Writers Guild Handbook*; and *ELSA, I Come With My Songs*, with Elsa Gidlow.

Introduction to Lady Clitoressa
& Her Circle

I t seems like everyone on the planet wants to court a lady: straight men, Lesbians, gay men — with many straight women considering it. No wonder. Womankind has always transcended hit-and-run "busy sex." We are profound artists in eroticizing sexuality with romance, sensuality and intimacy. Woman is also the happiness provider: food, the fine touches, cozy upkeep. This is because women tend to see themselves in terms of relationship or "interbeing." We value affinity, with full plumage of emotion. Women are apt to balance a relationship by negotiating rather than setting rules and procedures to protect their territory. Women choose quality and depth of sexual relationship over quantity, with little terror of commitment.

This is why two women together can be nectar to the nth degree, senses going beyond senses into mutually enfolding infinity. Even the word "Lesbian" is sensual, lithe, full of history and poetry. Studies of typical Lesbians (in non-clinical settings) show us to be happy, more independent and well-adjusted than heterocentric women. It has been said that Lesbians are among the true aristocracy in the United States, along with Native Americans. It certainly requires a form of personal aristocracy not to trade independence for marriage, or sexual favors for status, and to pursue a true partnership model rather than one of gender limitation and dominance. Lesbianism is much more than a lust for women or an exotic lifestyle, like yesterday's monocle or today's new wave haircut. Lesbianism is a politics and a philosophy of equality, of self-awareness and authenticity, of courage. There have long been circles of women freed by wealth or talent who invariably chose to cultivate woman-love and friendship. In the earlier half of this century, for example, the only closet such women would think of using was for their Chanel suits.

Coco Chanel was, after all, one of the sisters. Everyone who mattered knew. No one who mattered cared. Today, feminism and gay liberation have helped to create a similar freedom of consciousness for millions of women in all classes.

When my Lesbianism blossomed in the *apropos* year of 1969, I thought of it more as a revelation than a label. Thirsting for information on the "life," I talked with all the upcoming Lesbians I could and combed the libraries. It turned out there was less known about the bonding patterns of Lesbians than about those of bandicoots and bobolinks. Where was the Dian Fossey of dykedom? I ultimately found someone whom I can only call one of the Lesbian luminaries, a wise poet in her seventies. From England, by way of Montreal and New York City, she had overcome deep poverty and tragedy to create a Lesbian Avalon in the northern California redwoods. She laughed when we called her Lady Clitoressa. *Lady* originally meant "one who kneads the bread to lightness," and, of course, *clitoris* means "Goddess."

Her true name is Elsa Gidlow, a muse of *savoir-faire* and *savoir-vivre*. I filled notebooks with her. Be careful, they said, she is like Zen, she may break your heart. She did, of course, and then took care to teach me how hearts grow back. She has written her own autobiography, *ELSA, I Come with My Songs*, and, suffice it to say, to this bumptious new Lesbian she was an arch, yet compassionate, Ms. Manners. She believed Lesbians could use a guide not to "excruciatingly correct behavior," but to "ecstatically correct behavior." Elsa always said Lesbian feminist politics would mellow into "less bludgeoning." "Yes, Lesbianism is a slice of life, and yes, Lesbianism is a piece of cake."

Serve it forth. Our number and variety are legion. The most conservative, so of course most quoted, estimate and definition of Lesbians in the United States is from the old *Kinsey Reports* of the staid and fearful fifties: 10 percent of women. This means, minimally, twelve million Lesbians today in the United States. Hey, that's twenty-one Lesbians born every hour!

But we know Lesbians are made as well as born, especially since the great revolution in sexual imprinting which feminism began. Until harassment for sexual affinity ends, no census of us is possible. Gay researchers estimate there are two or three Lesbians for every one counted in surveys. Even this depends on how one defines Lesbianism.

Remember when a woman was defined as a person who was bounded on the north by her husband, on the east by her children,

12

on the south by her poverty and on the west by her clothes? Today, only 27 percent of households are "traditional" married couples with children. More than 25 percent of all Lesbians are mothers, and glad of that, if not of our poverty. Lesbians, like most women, still tend to be poor, but also to be well-educated, opting for jobs which provide independence, if not status and fat checks. Clothes? Lesbian fashion has always been the fashion of freedom.

To paraphrase Alice Walker, Lesbianism is to feminism as purple is to lavender, with Lesbianism itself an evolving, continuous spectrum of sensibilities. Some define a Lesbian as a woman whose deepest emotional, erotic and spiritual commitment and loyalty is to a woman or to women as a class. By this definition, most women are Lesbian, according to the latest *Hite Report* on women's sexuality. For women, erotic feeling brings into play *all* the senses, not strictly genital ones.

Some would define a Lesbian as an androgynous woman, whose gender roles of receptivity and of energy are well-mixed, who can "play" at sex roles but not get entangled in them. Women who are vulnerable and sassy, tough and forgiving. It is self-obsessed men who need to define Lesbians as she-males, as somehow being "in love against" them. Wanting men to want us sexually is what men want. The Lesbian holds a profound affection for her own female self and feels free to respond to this vitality and eroticism in all women. My favorite definition is, "A Lesbian is a woman who can teach you how to fix a car — or a cat." If one insists on defining Lesbians merely by genital performance (and who could be so simple?), well, go ahead. Lesbians do love pleasure for pleasure's sake. Let us be defined as the sex into orgasm, not wargasm.

The Lesbian agenda is a human agenda. Women are more conscious of the earth we inherited from our Mother and are borrowing for our children. Lesbian feminists have been at the forefront of virtually all the progressive movements of the last twenty years and more. We care about all beings' rights and futures, be they monkeys, marshes or rocks. Emma Goldman was right as usual: "Queer people are people who are sane in an insane society." The norm is not always normal. Lesbianism is one way of being committed to the life-force in a paternalistic culture of mega-death. Setting ourselves aside from the norm allows us to be creative. Our family networks aim for a climate of security and love; they are good models for small, self-sustaining communities. By making our stand for erotic, gender and personal freedom, Lesbians are living out the revolution every day. Lady Clitoressa once summed up her "Trinity of Lesbian Ethiquette":

13

1) Be true to your own life and love standards.
2) Avoid hurting others unnecessarily or exploiting anyone.
3) Try to prevent bad situations from getting worse.

Countless Lesbians from all parts of this country and abroad came to visit Lady Clitoressa's green pastures of conversation. They warmed to her Trinity; she especially warmed to their "sensual intellects." I thank many of these women who widened both my horizon and my heart, especially those in loving, but trenchant controversy with the "pride and prejudice" of this book. While we are into disclaimers, the *Advisor* is, yes, mainly drawn from Lesbians' viewpoints in this small golden crescent made up of San Francisco, Marin and Alameda counties in northern California. Here we live in a beautiful bubble, a psychic seaport with cosmic libido. "Can you come over and meditate?" "Your space or mine?" All I can do is invite you to visit. We will reserve the sky and the sea. Be prepared, though. San Francisco is the only city which asks, "Did you come?" To the light, liberty and levity of your answer.

It is now clear that we beautiful, proud faerie folk are not leaving the garden, that we are, in fact, multiplying. A Lesbian rainbow is smiling over this grassy star. On her lips is one word: *Change.*

Celeste West
San Francisco, 1989

I.
The Sweet
Arts:

Lesbian Flirting,
Courtship & Romance

L et us begin with flirting. Isn't that where it usually begins? Flirting is kindred to music, a light touch being both means and end. The word itself derives from the old French *fleureter*, literally "to move lightly from flower to flower." A form of flirting is cruising, more goal-oriented and assertive (*con brio*). Each Lesbian has her unique flirting style, with marvelous variations. In the beginning, you may want to learn, even rehearse, a few themes, or call them "opening plays" as in other field sports. Never fear; even if you feel terminally shy, you can still develop the quality of "eloquent receptivity," possibly the most magnetic of all seduction styles. Lesbians appreciate that shyness is often a veil for the virtues. Aggressiveness, naturally, is forbidden. Human beings who four-paw it are tolerated only in dim recesses of hetland.

Natalie Barney, the "American in Paris" whose brilliant art salons are legendary, holds Lesbiana's title, *"une seductive exemplaire."* Natalie devoted her considerable wealth and genius to friendship *amoureuse*, picking up women lovers at the beach well into her eighties. While her fluent bilingualism must have been captivating, one of Natalie's greatest charms was her capacity throughout life to blush like a novice upon being introduced to a desirable woman. Who would not be delighted by a compliment so roseate?

Flirting and cruising, also like music, improve with practice. There are few easy short-cuts, although accents and blushes do help. Consider using the following techniques, which we will discuss at length, as part of a repertoire: *clitzpah*; conversational foreplay; body language; knowledge of proven cruising places; and, for complete safety, a rejection survival kit.

Then, be prepared. Flirting and cruising may indeed open the gates to that ecstatic, full-blown yet fragile garden: Lesbian Romance and Courtship. Here the price of admission is giving up your safe boundaries and your workaday, ordinary mind. We go through the flower, into the psychedelic, pulsing, evanescent lavender petals of Romance, you are Queen to your Queen . . . Then, alas, isn't this also where things usually end? We wonder: what happened? Where does the flower of Romance go when she dies? Prolong her, you can. Preserve her, you cannot. Always comes the time to reseed. Thus, planting instructions for new romance between old partners are

17

included as we close this chapter. Remember to pause awhile, not only to marvel — but to rest. This is what cycles are for.

Clitzpah

Cruising *clitzpah* is the attitude of innocent hedonism: pleasure in/pleasure out. You are open, wide open, to a visitation of angels, here and now, without shame. *Clitzpah* is the give-a-little, get-a-little road to adventure. You feel worthy to be lavished with kisses — and to taste and treat a woman's body to the same. If you do not, you should. You are a child of the universe; now go cruising to celebrate. You have the divine (and First Amendment) right to gracefully propose anything you wish to a lady. You, of course, respect her supreme right of rejection, since you must occasionally invoke same. Rejection is, after all, one player who makes the courtship stakes so exciting. More on the shifting and valuable roles of rejection later. For now, celebrate *clitzpah*, that life-affirming jooce-on-the-loose, singing that we pass this way but once. Why not browse in passion and delight?

Finally, *clitzpah* is politically correct: A big strong feminist like you can't really be afraid to ask a sister to dance!

Conversational Foreplay

You don't have to worry so much about cruising conversation once the ball is in motion and both women are warmed up. Lesbian flirting, like lesbian seduction, is an exchange. No one controls. No one is quarry. The big challenge is to first indicate to a woman you want to volley with her in the court of delights. This stroke is called "openers." Review *clitzpah* and memorize *Lady Clitoressa's First Law of Motion: Nine times out of ten, YOU are going to have to make the first move.* In the cruising game, even the most stomping Lesbians play an amazingly comic, "After you, my dear Alphonse . . . " routine. Each woman waits for the other to begin, in one of the strangest mating rituals of all species. Shy, very shy, women lead more exciting lives than ordinary folk can ever imagine. What seems like a mere *tête-à-tête* to the bold is to the shy High Adventure, fraught with perils and dazzling successes. "I smiled at her, and she smiled back!" may last two weeks for us. It is a miracle Lesbians ever taste sweet pollen at all, but it all works out as it is supposed to . . . later or sooner. To make something happen now, simply work out a few general openers which feel natural to you. Practiced does not mean insincere. Virtually all the gentle rakes in Lady Clitoressa's Circle have some openers rehearsed.

As a rule, all agree that it is wise never to make your openers devastatingly witty, sarcastic or sophisticated. Your recipient usually can't come up with a quick repartee; she then feels clunky and wants to escape the situation — and you. A remark like, "Do you always have this much fun?" falls into this shoot-from-the-lips category. You want to frolic with this woman, not pin her to the wall. A lightly sexual innuendo like, "Can I buy you a drink — or a summer at Blue Fish Cove?" leaves many women flustered — even if they do know what the hell you're talking about. A starving artist, however, confessed to enjoying the irony of, "May I buy you a drink, or would you just like the money?" This all led to a fascinating exchange on art, women's economics, and onward . . . Here is a New Age opener: "Earth is such a beautiful place. Do you come here often?" which of course requires a most benevolent setting not to sound dippy.

It is a bit *outré* these days for Lesbians to make bar or party rounds plying alcohol like some kind of boozy big daddy. You have to catch a lady between glasses, and Lesbians are sipping slower these days or observing the ritual with mineral water or juice. If you must, ask to "get" (not "buy") her a drink, and of course pay for it. A hot player responds with a dazzling smile, "I'll get the next round," an incandescent player with, "Maybe we can have the next one some place quieter . . . " Here's a Twelve-Step opener: "If it is no longer romantic to be alcoholic, is it alcoholic to be romantic?" One good, all-around opener for anywhere, which doesn't depend on on drinking props, is to ask, "May I join you for a moment?" The "moment" disarms a lady who fears being stuck with a strange bird — and gives you a way out if you don't click.

The Circle's favorite opening for most occasions is the friendly, "How are you doing?" No risk to you, unthreatening to her. A few women will begin to tell you — in specific detail. With your appreciative listening ("Oh. Oh? Oh!" if you are momentarily tongue-tied), the conversation leaps forward, unless of course she happens to be in some kind of misery beyond hope. Then you dive for the restroom. Most women, however, offer the usual "Fine/O.K." and inquire the same. Even if she doesn't inquire, here is the big lead-in for your first gambit past openers to real dialogue. Offer any variation of "Well, I'm feeling good because of . . . " Here mention any little daily delight, recent coup, or pleasant commentary on the scene. You appear interesting, successful, or at least positive — not someone to run away from. "I just sold a story" . . . "got a bike for touring" . . . "saw a wonderful film" . . . "agree with what the panel pointed out" . . . and so forth. You can describe a job incident in order to steer the conversation back to her asking, "What do you do?" since most women do something. Women may have boring jobs, so the best query is, "How do you like to spend your time?" Notice that as soon as you say something flattering about her appearance or clothing — and compliments are excellent openers — you have quickly signaled that your interest is probably more than, well, sisterly. Ask her opinion of *anything*. Somewhere in this introductory chat-up, be sure to insert a cordial, "By the way, my name is . . . "

Granted, this may not sweep a woman off her feet, but we're talking first base here: how a world series begins. The vital purpose of all ritual social phrases and "weather" small talk is *contact*; content is virtually irrelevant. Small talk announces, "I am friendly and I want to acknowledge this moment we have together in the world." Small talk is a light intermission from the literal. You too can lighten up if you just remember we are in the pleasant land of process here, not content. Things warm up easily if you can somehow discover a common interest, which is why meeting at a women's studies course or a gardening class is better than meeting at a bar or on the bus. Never immediately and sweepingly cross-examine a woman in a "what is your life story" query on things like personal goals, obstacles, parents, coming out, or previous lovers. You are dying to know, but instant intrusiveness is an invasion of privacy. First, share a couple of your own broad interests with anecdotes (food, cats, current events, women's issues). To get information, give information; then things begin to flow.

If all your attempts as Lady Chatterley continue to draw silence, remember purple xx chromosomes do not necessarily rapport make. Be patient, however, with brilliant flashes of silence. It is uncluttered awareness. At a silent "stalemate," simply enjoy being with a beautiful woman. Smile at her for as long as it would take to say, "Would you like to make love beyond words?" Silence doesn't cost anything and it doesn't hurt. It provides refreshment. Breathe in well-being and exhale hope. Remember this lady may have just ventured out from Goddess knows where and may need a chance to sort through suddenly new options — like you. If, however, she is not playing, period, have the *galanterie* to say, "Well, I've enjoyed talking to you." Ova and out.

The most important quality in conversational foreplay is the good energy of being there, alive and enjoying the game. This brings us to *Lady Clitoressa's Second Law of Motion: Exhibit no undue haste.* Lesbians have whole constellations of erotic emotions and senses to bring into play. It is not only *gauche* to move toward instant gratification, it is foolhardy. Most Lesbians resent and mistrust a rushed, fixated demand for sex from a stranger. Unlike victims of raging testosterone, we can afford to be connoisseurs of subtlety, to be tantric with time. Sensuous Lesbians know half the fun is getting there; the blossoms of ardor grow in the season of anticipation. We say, "familiarity brings attempt." At first meeting, try for a date, not a feel. "I'd really be interested in getting together again. May I call you?" Or, less vaguely, "I'm going to the women's art exhibit. I'd like to go with you. If you're free, would you like to come?" Here, you are an active person *already* going to do something interesting. You are presenting a neutral-sounding opportunity. An event-date can feel less vulnerable than asking a woman to dinner or to a dance, which more clearly indicates romantic interest. Whatever your pace, do something. Don't thin your blood with "might have beens"; any action may bloom, or at least achieve closure. Go ahead and catch the wheel of karma as it turns.

Let us say you have moved the wheel forward. We come to the next step along the path of conversational foreplay after "openings," after the great warm-up. It is the hot stroke called "making the move," the proposition for s-e-x. Making the move can be attempted at first sight or on the fiftieth date, depending on your period, sign of the zodiac, and the signals you are getting. You may be propositioning this woman for life or for one sweet night. Practice this challenging scenario: it is your last night in Minneapolis. You've been chatting up your seemingly interested beauty all evening and it is getting late. Playfully, you touch hands. "I hate to go." Then your fingers attentively caress each tip of hers in a silent conversation. Before your very eyes her nipples harden to salute yours. It is now or never. But *who* will make the move???

You remember the odds: she may be one of the nine Lesbians in ten with only budding *clitzpah*. The odds clearly dictate: it's YOUR move. Summoning all the *délicatesse* of Lady C's "no undue haste" that you can possibly muster since time *is* actually running out, you slowly whisper, "May I kiss you just once?" [Success, long slow success. Deep glance and moisten lips appreciatively to . . .]

21

"I would love to kiss you all over *sometime.*" [Loving smile. Breathe deeply.] "You know I would be delighted *if you could* spend the night with me . . . "

Serious seducers will note the harmless-sounding "just once" of the opening line and the open-ended "sometime" of the next. You are not, after all, desperate. One kiss *is* better than none and sometime *is* better than never. "If you could" in the final proposition gives the lady who is not currently ready a way to respond with her diplomatic "Why, I can't," rather than "I won't."

The idea here is not to provide generic, canned come-ons, only to emphasize old-fashioned, fragrant good manners and the subtlety for which Lesbians are famous. In the above scenario, the qualifying phrases weave lacy loopholes for both players to dance through. You can easily reach out and you can easily let go. Perhaps *this* time, you will have to let *this* woman go. It is, however, *always* a successful advance to gracefully let a beautiful woman know you are, well, moist. She can at least enjoy the compliment, while you enjoy sharing your sweet life pulse. You have passed Lesbian Cruising 101, where the only failure is not to try.

Unlike gay men, Lesbians aren't programmed to use code phrases for making the move. At a bar, "Do you live near here?" is a somewhat common signal, and is information strategy in any case. Do spare us "How do you like your eggs in the morning?" and the flustered old "Your face or mine?" Women with Mercury in Scorpio have been known to fall for "Do you want to steal away?" Lady Clitoressa herself was swept into sweetness by "Marry me for tonight," a night which lasted for thirteen years. Naturally, sex discussions, whether sociological or downright torrid, are often used to desensitize the topic and quicken the move. "Aural intercourse" is fun in itself for learning the varieties of Lesbian sex. It is essential if any exotic proclivities are sought. Moreover, since AIDS, we must learn to discuss sex practices and sex histories with prospective partners.

Many women have asked about the old back-pocket hanky color code as a short-cut signal of sexual openness and preferred variety. Since Lesbians are skilled generalists, few of us ever learn what color bandanna stands for which proffered technique. Suffice it to say that a colored bandanna in a back pocket usually means, "You don't have to wonder and can cut the prelims; I'm in the mood for the old rock and roll." A hanky may also signal the lady is not fluent in the native language — or just has a head cold. So you had better find out. Hey, an opener! Flourish a purple bandanna in a back pocket yourself and see what happens . . .

Body Language

If the previous section on conversation seems rather prosaic, it is because you cruise with your whole body. In the beginnings of the social dance, what you say is rarely as important as *how*. The body electric is so communicative that, in fact, most messages we receive are non-verbal. Remember the era of the sexy smoker? She never had to use words to strike the first match. In general, try not to begin verbally cruising a lady until her antennae are out. The Lesbian mating ritual can involve subtle signals, even telepathy, and energy fields. Use them.

Many Lesbian seduction artists begin with the eyes. Again and again, Natalie Barney's *amies* speak of first being captivated, sometimes even ravished, by her incomparable eyes. One glance was an intimate personal exchange. She remarked, "Anyone can touch. It is the optic nerve that sears the soul." If this is too poetic for you, a "scientific" study quoted in *Sex: A Users Manual* found 62 percent in a national poll said eyes most attracted them, with hair a poor second at 22 percent. Truly, "to hear with the eyes belongs to love's fine wit."

One reason bars may feel sexy is because of all the visual appraisal and the eye-to-eye games going on. The eyes are upturned cups. Pupils widen in dim light as they do in desire. As two Lesbians begin to shine it on, a flashing eye game may begin what we call the "applause response." First, you see yourself mirrored approvingly in a woman's eyes. Pleased, you flash back your image of her as being a discerning, sensitive soul. She sees this attractive reflection and flashes an even more delighted view of you back. The applauding images mirror each other mirroring each other like drops of shining dew on a spider's net. What ultimately becomes of this exquisite, fragile illusion only time will tell. It is an entrancing way to begin.

As magical as dancing with mirrors is, the eye is also an ancient symbol of honesty, clarity and power. Avalokiteshvara, who became the beloved Chinese Goddess Kwan Yin, is sometimes portrayed with a thousand open hands, each with an eye. The Ladies say, "The difference between making love with a man or making love with a woman is like the difference between having your eyes closed or your eyes open." Women often position themselves across from one another to be able to look at one another. Two men are likely to prefer sitting side to side. One pioneering study of the Lesbian experience is called, for good reason, *Look Me in the Eye*. With prolonged eye contact, you can signal to a woman that you desire her, whether across a bar or a crowded classroom. Yes, it does take practice to hold your gaze appreciatively when a woman notices; we usually lower our eyes quickly when caught in someone's space. But you are shameless — and friendly. Raise your eyebrows and smile softly. No smirks, please. Lady Clitoressa usually polishes off the exchange with an almost imperceptible bow. "The only etiquette one need ever know is how to bow from the heart." Along with a nod or smile, you can wing the lady a silent greeting, a warm color, a touch of faerie dust. Some smoothies even get away with a touch to their hat brim.

To ease into all of this, a little exercise: practice winking at women who pass in the street walking or in cars. Just wink, no leers, not a word, not even a smile. Drivers, ticket takers, telephone lineswomen at work are quite safe. Police officers are really fun, not to mention nuns. The women can never be sure you committed the rakish act. Should she actually demand, "Did you wink at me?", smile and with friendly surprise ask, "Wink? Should I have?" Winks are disarming and conspiratorial when done with agility. This is why they are extremely useful when caught doing something naughty, like photocopying *A Lesbian Love Advisor* at the office.

When meeting a lovely lady and pursuing eye-to-eye contact, do not proceed relentlessly like some est graduate, but with a lambent touch-and-go. Timing is everything. You can tell when you have invaded. A woman will sometimes turn her whole head like she has been struck. Different cultures have different eye etiquette. Friendly eye contact to a Caucasian may be rude to an Asian. One study reported that whites tend to make eye contact while listening, Blacks while talking, giving white people the erroneous impression Blacks aren't listening.

Eyes are only one romantic gateway. Blind women, for example, have a way of listening with their whole body that is a marvel of eloquent receptivity from which we could all learn. Margaret Mead, recently revealed adept of Lesbian sensibility, is said to have often held her palms upward and open during a private conversation. Calm, complete stillness means, "I am receptive." Let your blood beat, and she will hear it. This is the quality of *être là*, being here with brilliant intensity. Skilled seductives (and sages) use a whole range of active listening tools such as eye contact, leaning forward, synchronizing breath, nodding, reaching out (at an especially touching moment), and above all, *never* interrupting. Nor do they ever speed up the conversation, finishing another's sentences in Type A behavior. Why hurry the dance?

Space is another delicate consideration for the cruiser. We all know "space" for a Lesbian feminist is as vital as breathing. All women (in fact, all cultures) have different "comfort spaces" on meeting a new person. Even men know this; ruthless ones try to dominate it. Begin at least a couple of feet away and circle in depending on a woman's cues. If you are both sitting, distance is less threatening and you can "lean" into the conversation for closeness. Hugging is a great study in space dynamics. A typical non-hugger, when pressed, does not move in, but leans into the hug at an acute angle. This is known as the "A-frame hug." Be alert — you have got a "space case" here; be as careful as if you were with a wild deer. Big huggers lead with the whole body and trade breast-to-breast and delta-dawn closeness. Don't assume this is sexual. Some women are munificent with physical affection, as are some cultures. It has been found that the more peace-loving a culture, the more it is able to demonstrate physical affection. Three guesses whether Maggie Thatcher or Nancy Reagan are big huggers? Medium huggers will move in, but slightly deflect the body in an almost left to right hip hug.

Shaking hands upon meeting is another fascinating study. It comes naturally to some women and not to others. European Lesbians seem born with the tendency. The French are utterly charming, often shaking with the left hand, "nearer the heart." A naughty variation is to lower your lips to the back of her hand, then turn it over, blowing gently on the erotically sensitive inside of her wrist. Simply shaking hands can be very powerful if accompanied by looking directly into a woman's eyes and pausing for a moment. Be prepared to diffuse that advance with a mild-mannered remark. Yes, it is proper to shake hands with your gloves on, but why should a Lesbian deny herself?

Where Did You Meet Her?

Clitzpah is not all sensual assertiveness and *savoir-faire*. It is also smarts. *Where* to pick up Ms. Right? A wild lesberado bar? Wrong. Even lifelong members of the drinking class in Lady Clitoressa's Circle says bars are an inefficient world of trivial pursuit. Go to a bar to visit with friends, listen to music, relax, dance, play pool, look at beautiful women doing all of the above — even smoke a bar drink at a 500 percent mark-up while you're at it. But remember *Lady Clitoressa's Law of Fluids: A romance begun in a bar will end in a bar.* Bars tend to attract cruising drinkers who, relying on Dutch courage, are altering their realities drink by drink. You can't be sure of anything, especially if you are loaded yourself. True, new Lesbians just off the boat and a few on the wagon abound in bars, but they are probably as shy as you are.

Alcohol, unlike some mood enhancers, lowers your quality control and sensitivity. Worst of all, you may drink yourself into an aspic from nervousness, end up in bed like a bad joke and have a bone-crushing hangover to boot. This is romance? Las Vegas odds apply to the possibility of abiding love peeping over the rim of a glass. We can recommend bars only because they are dark, sexy and anonymous, like the one-night stands they are sometimes good for.

The world-class way to cruise is to meet a love via common interests: workshops, politics, spiritual practice, sports, classes, readings, work, hobbies. (Whatever happened to hobbies?) Even if you do not instantly meet anyone sexually exciting and available here, your time is still well invested doing something valuable, *sans* bar tab, smoky clothes and frustration. You have become more attractive, finding new knowledge, a community, a friend or worthwhile connection. Maybe you will even discover it is not a lover you currently need, but social pleasures and support. Women's coffee houses, bookstores, various women's centers (health, professional, gymnastic) are good cruising because they are often highly Lesbian.

Large parties and dances are a bit like bars for cruising if liquor and Lesbians are the only common ingredients. Smaller dinner parties with friends and new women are much better because conversation is less superficial, you can get background info on your quest, and you usually have a good time even if no new sexual liaison is immediately begun. Lesbian friends are usually great matchmakers, being romantics themselves, so ask your buddies to help set up dinners or "double dates." You'll do the same for them once you get married if they go back on the stroll.

Speaking of the stroll, did you ever wonder why some Lesbians never go anywhere without their dogs? Dogs can cheerfully provide an excellent way to meet new women — women who love dogs, of course, and some Lesbians would have it no other way. The dog instantly breaks the ice, and you can move from canine discussions to those of the human species. Cat-loving Lesbians can proceed directly to their pets for instruction. Meditate on this wild, joyfully purring maven of seduction to see how it is *really* done.

A member of Lady Clitoressa's Circle admits to another ploy. She answers Lesbian "apartment share" notices to meet women, especially when new to a community. With a prospective roomie, you can get down fast, find out if she's single, and instantly evaluate her general tastes and lifestyle. After the room deal "falls through," wait a couple of days and ask her to coffee. If successful, make sure you are a damn good lover in every way, and sin no more. Our itinerant friend usually confesses down the line, "Your candid, witty rent notice just undid me," which is probably true. She is forgiven. Morality, of course, forbids you to lure a needy house seeker into your den, unless of course you have an extra room to rent.

Certain avocations are lucrative Lesbian hunting grounds. Set up some beloved side "career" in freelance writing or anything to do with publishing, music, the occults, photography, body work — almost any service or art where you control the hours and can meet new women as an equal. Many side vocations pay more in people-meeting than in cash, but the Ladies say orgasms with a tax write-off have special *frisson*. Making sexual come-ons to a more vulnerable client by an empowered professional — doctor, therapist, spiritual advisor, teacher — is an overwhelmingly male phenomenon and abhorred in Lesbian culture. This discussion is about pleasure/with, not power/over.

In large cities and college towns there are often shifting organizations formed solely for Lesbian socializing. The famous Daughters of Bilitis was the Grandmamma of them all. Social organizations' notices appear in women's papers. If you don't see one of your choice, you can always begin a group. If all local papers are straight and male, you can use discreet wording to get the idea across. Rural Lesbians, near a town with one movie theater, organized a regular "Ladies' Night." Lesbian youth groups ("teen women") pop up while the organizers wait to get I.D.'s. The rise of Lesbian sororities on college campuses is knocking everybody's socks off. "Lesbians Over Forty" was so successful in San Francisco that "Slightly Older Lesbians" was founded by ladies-in-waiting for the Big Four-O. All these groups inspired San Francisco comedian Linda Moaks to found the "So-So's," the "Slightly Older Sex Objects," a name which illustrates the mood of a purely social group with hit-or-miss common interests.

Playing the Personals

One of the best ways to target a prospective lover, or at least practice doing so, is via the classified "personals." These are yet another form of self-publishing to gain respectability. Personals even got a rave

Ms. Magazine article, whose own classifieds (now defunct) could have used a bit of tarting up. Actually, it was a woman who ran the first personal in 1727. She got a month in the loony bin — where she probably met someone exciting. One of the largest, most captivating set of Lesbian classifieds may run as long as a full page in San Francisco's *Bay Times* (formerly *Coming Up!*) newspaper. These are beloved in the community for their wit, poignancy, and, yup, creme-of-the-dream sex talk. You can also get the Lesbian *Wishing Well Magazine* and *Golden Threads* for women over fifty. To take a walk on the wild side, use the Lesbian erotic magazines *On Our Backs, Bad Attitude*, and, for the s & m follies, *Outrageous Women. New York Review of Books, Village Voice*, and *The Nation* as well as some city entertainment weeklies will publish Lesbian personals, but the male response is deafening. We keep hoping *The Celibate Woman* will run chakra leads.*

Whatever your venue, gone is the loser image of a lonely weirdo placing an ad. Lesbian writers tend to sound eloquent, attractive and refreshingly clear about what they want. Style varies with community: acceptable in San Francisco or *On Our Backs* may sound a little wild and wacko elsewhere. Writers are far from wallflowers, but usually woman who find bars dreary, and are too busy to cruise haphazardly (moms, career achievers), or are fed up with boring or pointless preliminaries. Some are women in transition, new to the community or to the dating game. A gay techster in Lady Clitoressa's Circle says there is also gay computer sex, electronic bulletin boards where you can post come-ons. It seems, however, the testosterone level is so high and the kink so heavy that Lesbian contacts (bauds?) are not playing much.

I girded my loins to place an ad when there were other successes in Lady Clitoressa's Circle at playing the personals. It took days for this once intrepid reporter to perk up her picas. Here is what I learned. The dread act itself of compiling an ad is valuable, even if one never runs it. It is at least as good as paying a therapist to get you to define your immediate and future goals in order to quit futzing around. To carefully compose your precious identity in a few words, to state what you care about in this life and what you need from another human being, is a great way to pull up your socks and get moving in the right direction. How honest do you dare to be about

---

* *Bad Attitude*, Box 110, Cambridge, MA 02139; *Bay Times*, 592 Castro, San Francisco, CA 94114; *The Celibate Woman*, 3306 Ross Place, N.W., Washington, DC 20008; *Golden Threads*, Box 2416, Quincy, MA 02269; *On Our Backs*, 526 Castro, San Francisco, CA 94114; *Outrageous Women*, Box 23, Somerville, MA 02143; *Wishing Well Magazine*, Box 117, Novato, CA 94948.

your real needs? Will you present your authentic self or the glass ego which shatters when the Ninety-Day Romance Warranty is over? Will you heal narrowing, raw prejudices like, "no fats, fems or forties"? Or will your ad bestow self-love by showing you how decent and desirable you really are?

So much for know thyself; on to the technique of writing hot copy. You have more control if you place an ad, rather than answer someone else's specifications. So for heaven's sake, be *specific* about what you want! Sure, we all are taught to want someone "hot and sexy," but what I realized while I was writing was that what I really want is a witty, cheerful woman of the world who owns her own business or is an artist or activist type. This *makes* her hot and sexy to me. If you specifically require a college grad, a fuck-buddy, a monogamist, a clean and sober, or elegant wrapping, say so! A "want list" is clearer and sounds much better than negative "none of this" grumpiness.

Spell out your main interests, your favorite ways of spending quality time with another woman: backpacking, music, fireside sex, Scrabble. Present a brief physical/personality/approach-to-life description of yourself or the ad lacks flesh. In this, be as enticingly honest as you can. Misrepresentation sets you up for rejection. If you feel you have an important disability, mention it, and don't apologize. This way you avoid the nerve-wracking wait for a proper context for discussion. People lie most often about appearance. Happily Lesbians aren't as much into *cliché* looksism as the het set is. Above all, *use* humor. Don't merely announce that you have a great sense thereof. In all strong, active writing, a verb job is best; hold every adjective up to the light and eliminate wishy-washy words like "somewhat," "sort of," "slightly," and irrelevant lines like, "I've never done this before." If one more Lesbian in San Francisco writes that she likes to walk on the beach, we are sending her to Kansas.

Use a sparky headline even if your ad is serious. Here are a few to get you in the mood: "Cunning Linguist Seeks Loving Conversations," "Deadly Top or Breath-Taking Bottom?" "Whatever Happened to Sex?" "Jump Start My Heart," "Looking for a Custom-Made Relationship in an Off-the-Rack World?" "Let's Do It 'til We Drop!" "Pushy Femme Seeks Soft Butch," "Crazed Hussy Seeks Same," "Let's Meet Minds and Mons." This is the shortest ad on record at *Coming Up!* "I Want to Fuck! You're a dyke. I'm a dyke. Reply CU Box FB2." It got a huge response.

Never give your phone number; crazy, very crazy, men will call. Use a post office or the paper's box service. When you get a likely response, have a phone conversation for mutual screening, then meet in a public place. Luckily, we are not dealing with men, or the list of precautions could now become endless. Rehearse having "an appointment" right after the date in case you have to make a quick getaway.

Some ideas for successfully responding to an ad: answer if it really charms you even if you don't meet every detailed qualification. Most writers will give you a little slack; I made an exception to my non-smoking rule for a pipe smoker and a woman who rolled her own with one hand. Explain precisely which unique qualities of the ad attracted you. Too much flattery is never enough; we are talking courtship here. The writer will appreciate the reassurance even if she's an old hand at the personals. Offer a short description of yourself, with a photo looking happy and approachable. Oddly enough, if you are too gorgeous, you may scare women away. More than looks, a photo reveals the "image" a woman likes of herself. Do you choose to pose with a cat, a Harley or with the light and shadow on your Hepburn cheekbones? Handwriting tantalizes too, so don't type your *billets doux*. To receive a response on a dot-matrix printer is about as romantic as receiving plastic flowers. Above all, sound upbeat. You are looking for a lover, not a therapist. Respond in the same style as the ad: serious to serious, playful to playful, erotic to erotic. A good ad will get a huge response, so answer quickly, and do not be surprised if your fantasy woman is too busy to get back to you.

Here is the first ad I wrote. I am not a member of the "keep it short" school. We're looking for depth here, at mere pennies a word. Since quantity was not my aim, I discouraged s & m'ers, Tories, and smokeys. I also lost all the women who are not horse lovers, but can they matter? All I can say is life was never the same after:

Rendezvous at the O.K. Corral

This gallant, thoroughbred Sagittarian is looking for a she-stallion to curry with friendship, perhaps lather with love. I'm a long-distance runner, winner of the Lesbian Triple Crown with three previous long-term relationships to season my savvy and open my heart. (References upon request.) A happily eccentric, almost financially "stable" writer (who's ever secure, anyway?), I like a big meadow and accord you the same. When we share passion, I can love you gentle or wild — no spurs or whips, natch. S & S (sex and spirituality) can take us to the Circle of Roses. My racing silks are the colors of anarchy; I am an ardent, cheerful lefty: 90 percent politically aware; 10 percent plain sleazy. Are you my five-gaited/twelve-stepping/non-smoking/self-accepting laughing Zen cavalier? Have you learned comedy the hard way? Are you a right-livelihood entrepreneur or activist? Since I am a silver-maned 45-year-old, with my boho elegance becoming more dashing by the moment, why wait

to horse around with this centaur woman? Photo, neigh, Beauty and courage are
more important than looks, but a silver tongue, now . . .

I got twenty-five responses, six of which were smashing. I galloped out on five lovely dates. The sixth response was from my former lover who recognized me and thought I had written the ad expressly for her. She is a Leo for whom the world turns . . . We got over a lot of old garbage, and came back together. So try the personals before you spend all that money on couple counseling.

The Rejection Survival Kit

Here we arrive, as we must, at *Lady Clitoressa's Law of Gravity: The roots of rejection are infinite*. Please recognize that while you may take a cruising rejection personally, it simply cannot be offered that way. This woman does not, after all, even *know* you personally. True, she may not be attracted to your appearance, personality type, or electro/magnetic/chemical fields. No one is everybody's type, but — ah — everybody is someone's. The woman you happen to choose to pursue (based on your own "type" bias) may be tired, busy, depressed, with someone, needing to be "alone in a crowd"; the possibilities are — well, infinite. You can play only your own hand.

Talented cruisers plying a large heterogeneous group say that if they are not turned down a couple of times in one evening, they are not really trying. The key is never to dwell on "why," but keep moving. As musician Laurie Anderson says, "It's not the bullet that kills you, it's the hole." Don't let yourself be shell-shocked by a trivial "no" that has nothing to do with your true worth as a human being, let alone any basic survival needs. Trust perspective to Miss Manners, who reminds us, "excruciating moments are transitory." Miss Manners herself once publicly, in front of a whole audience, rejected the proffered hug of sweet love guru Leo Buscaglia. Buscaglia later turned it into such a delightful story that surely he, and even Miss Manners, is glad the entire episode happened exactly as it did. Each one of them simply had a different preferred scenario. At a given moment, someone you want contact with may have totally different plans. This will be a disappointment, but is hardly a devastating rejection of your soul.

Clearly, the more you cruise, the more rejections you garner. By trying it at all, you put yourself in a risk category. You will collect "noes," along with all the "maybes" and "yeses." This is a minimal

31

price to pay for tasting those delicacies which remain forever a fantasy to the less adventuresome. In the sweet arts, you live like an epicurean only if you can afford to lose like a stoic. In Zen Buddhism, when you ask someone to be your teacher, tradition dictates that she or he turn you down three times. The religion of Romance is no less rigorous. Since you are going to be collecting rejections anyway, be sure to try for the best prize in the house. Why reject yourself before she does? Your stunning choice may intimidate everyone and be the loneliest person in the room. Never settle for someone you think you are doing a favor. She has a right to be as haughty and discriminating as the ostensible queen of the hop. It is downright discouraging to be discarded by someone you didn't want in the first place, but it serves you right for being patronizing.

One of the most graceful things about skilled cruisers is that they never rudely turn down a pass themselves. They've been there. There is only one way to reject somebody: firmly and *cordially*. Smile when you say, "I'm just not interested tonight, but thanks for being friendly." You can even talk for a few minutes more. It doesn't cost anything to show you appreciate her taste and wish her well. Lesbians don't tend to be crudely persistent. It is especially rude to refuse to dance with any sober woman who invites you to — unless, of course, you don't know how, are incapacitated, or are deep in an absolutely critical conversation. If you are with a date, ask your date if she minds if you have one dance, saying you'll be right back. It is always easy, even pleasant, to dance one dance. Afterwards, genuinely thank your partner and depart the floor. She has not, after all, asked you to marry her. Whenever I see a lovely woman and good dancer abruptly turned down, I wonder what has happened to sisterhood? What has happened to the dance of life?

Romance, or Love as Madness

Leaving the valley of rejection, with a little pluck and perseverance you can ultimately climb to the wild highlands of Lesbian Romance & Courtship. These are not to be confused with the rich plateaus of Commitment. Romance is a fine madness if you know precisely what is going on and can smile at its excesses and absurdities. Romance comes in two general forms: *High Romance* and *Torment-Me Romance*. Both involve altered states of consciousness and magnificent obsessions. It is advised you have some sort of spirit-guide or friend to center you when the ride gets out of control, since

32

going beyond your usual boundaries is the whole point of romance. High Romance involves a ravishing play of the senses. These are virtually stripped, freed of daily sludge to become highly receptive and sensitive. Music can move you to tears, lyrics have layers of meaning, food is divine, wine jeweled, flowers become worlds of sensuality. Sex is sheer abandonment, the body quicksilver and honey. The body may also fluster a bit drunkenly, with blushing and pounding heart. The Ladies say the experience is much like taking the purest acid or potent hashish. You are open, on, at last empowered to drench yourself in beauty and meaning. Petty problems and chores don't exist or can be short-cut, barriers are down as you are called into great union. Disarmed, you are vulnerable, suggestible.

The analytical brain can merely try to fathom it all. Studies on brain pleasure centers show that during romantic infatuation, the body manufactures mood-enhancing drugs like the famous "love potion" amphetamine PEA (phenylethylamine). Lesbians, surely the most romantic creatures on earth, are perhaps super-synthesizers of PEA. Or is it the other way around — PEA nudges us into Lesbianism? One scientific explanation leads always to more questions. We do know an amphetamine like PEA causes a physical "rush" of high alertness and intensity, even sleeplessness or lack of appetite. The body also produces its own family of tranquilizing opiate drugs, "happiness hormones" like the famous endorphins. There has been major publicity, indeed new industries created, because aerobic exercise joyfully stimulates one's endorphin level. Depressives and people who tend to become addicted to any form of mood enhancer have often been found to be poorer natural alchemists of "in-house" drugs like PEA and the endorphins. Worse, whatever "prescriptives" exist within them can be destroyed by outside chemicals. Body alchemy can also be dramatically altered with diet, exercise and soul care. Now we know our semi-voluntary trips on the road to romance have similar effects.

The wonderful world of chemistry holds more romance news. Studies show the subtle chemical perfumes called "pheromones," which are found in all the body's secretions (perspiration, sex, urine), are likely to arouse women sexually more than they do men; men tend to become aggressive in the presence of these subconsciously sensed pheromones. Women also have keener senses of smell than men, especially at ovulation. Each Lesbian's own subtle fragrance comes from her pheromones, and each potion is as unique in the world as her fingertips. Like preferences in perfume, pheromone scents decidedly please or offend us. Initially, you may be captivated solely by a woman's pheromone scent, or by what it becomes blended with purchased perfume. If you later find you have absolutely no affinity with this woman and lament, "What could I ever have seen in her?", scent could be the subliminal siren. Pheromones can likewise be initial repellents to someone who should logically be perfect for you. Chemists who are "fragrance technicians" have synthesized insect pheromones to use them as traps or repellents, and are now researching synthetic human pheromones to use in human behavior modification. Very scary. The commercial perfume makers blatantly promising mood alteration seem benign by comparison. So, if you meet someone in the "chemically free space," which is becoming de rigueur in feminist circles, maybe this new relationship will be less confusing.

Scientific studies of romance neurochemistry suggest *how* our senses and brain pleasure centers fire up whirlpools of electrochemical magnetism. This materialist analysis cannot, however, explain the ultimate source or purpose of even an initial chemical reaction. It can never fully analyze the continuously moving interplay of the myriad subtleties operating beyond controlled laboratory conditions. Tunnel-visioned science does not have the tools to understand Lesbian romance — dare it try. Most Lesbians agree, however, with a prevailing scientific theory that romance exists in all its colors and fragrance for one ultimate purpose: procreation. All the Ladies agree that one good Lesbian romancer can create another Lesbian without so much as a generation gap. It takes only one deep kiss.

The entire world is a swirling laboratory of love when a woman is ready. Her move toward Lesbianism may be the scent of a flower on the night, the pull of the moon in her seasons, an awakened memory, a rekindled hope, a generous touch, a flash of the eyes . . . A woman may merely notice the magic of another woman, or she may allow herself to deeply taste the moment, or she may unreservedly draw the magic into every cell. Whatever her depth of involvement, most women, in the one poll we'd like to see, agree with Virginia Woolf: "It is women alone who capture my imagination." Since women are more conscious, we are more conscious of one another.

The beat of Lesbian romance loves to pulse itself on and on for the sheer joy of feeling good and alive. Be aware you encourage this cosmic élan vital by using certain amplifications such as drenching yourself in nature's bounty or exploring sensory gratifications and ritual with deep focus. If you pursue such things with your woman you will surely be swept on strong, wild currents of consciousness which some call madness because it is such super-sensory reality.

You may be irresponsible, sacrificing everything to passion. The state is ecstatic, but exhausting; no one can sustain it without pause. It usually peaks anywhere from a week to six months to two years, being more stimulating than nourishing. Some Lesbians, like the bewitching Margaret Anderson of the *Little Review*, who first published sections of James Joyce's *Ulysses* and became a courtroom *célèbre*, are no strangers to life's banquet. Margaret Anderson reported being slightly "romanced" by *everything* and wrote a passionate autobiographical trilogy about this exalted state. No Lesbian lover, artist, mystic or wit should miss her revelations.

While some like it *haute*, some do not. A few Lesbians prefer serenity of mind and rarely elect to experience *la folie à deux*. They choose their partners pragmatically like a Jane Austen heroine. Still others prefer a variation of High Romance called "Torment-Me." This preference shares many of the same sensory effects of High Romance. In Torment-Me, however, distance, not closeness, is the goal. The key to excitement and passion is a desperate yearning for an impossible love in a landscape of longing never to be relieved. The beloved is to be idealized, contemplated, suffered for, or forgiven. Indifference, betrayals, and persecution are endured. Torment-Me's are ingenious; if the romance begins to actually go well, a cast of competitors is often created or some other danger is manufactured to turn the torture level back up. A clucking audience is usually an essential ingredient for the whole painful drama. Great *angst* upon the land makes Torment-Me's feel alive, and, well — happy. One physical variant of Torment-Me can be s & m.

A younger, or more innocent, version of Torment-Me is called "The Crush." Here the object of affection is truly unavailable and probably always will be (teacher, celebrity, straight). Often, a romantic Lesbian crush is too innocent of carnal knowledge to focus on physical consummation.

Torment-Me Romance has a long and celebrated history in western civilization, beginning with the twelfth century tradition of Courtly Love. It is liberally lashed with Christian sadomasochism: pleasure must "hurt" to be worthy; suffering is ennobling; spirit is good, flesh evil. The essence of Torment-Me is its low-risk factor. You cannot lose the one you never had, you don't need to work at keeping her, you never even have to come out to the world. Torment-Me romantics have rich, if vainglorious, fantasy lives. They often excel in poetry and song writing.

Courtship Deportment

In romantic courtship, the goal is the other woman, period. If the cycle moves into love and commitment, the goal will spiral to become mutual happiness and each woman's spiritual growth. The plain romantic, however, can temper her sheer egoism by understanding it. Romantic love is your fantasy-partner idealization projected onto a woman you have recently met. You are psychologically distanced from her authenticity by your shining image of a make-believe woman. Meanwhile, she is rapturously doing the same thing to you. This is the "applause response" again. You are in love with love and yourself, not another person. Or as one wisehead remarked, "Whenever two women meet there are really eight women present. There is each woman as she sees herself, each woman as the other woman sees her, each woman as she reacts to the force-field of this particular woman, and each woman as she really is." This is all fine because people actually transform their ordinary grumpy selves into well-directed dream people, causing true pleasure on earth. Courtship is also the catalyst in the alchemy that may transmute the dross of selfish love into the gold of a giving love. Romance is the inspiration, the muse of love. Many of its silky ways must become practiced skills if a committed relationship is to flourish. Why should courtly honor and delight ever end?

Margaret Anderson makes dozens of suggestions for delicious deportment in courtship. The following list of romantic emanations include a few of Margaret's as well as favorites from Lady Clitoressa's Circle. Even something as potent as Lesbian sex or deep friendship will wither without romance's light. Note *Lady Clitoressa's Lunar Law: Love is like the moon; when it doesn't increase, it decreases.* Recognize that, too, all great friendships are at least slightly *amoureuses* with consensual flirting. Each woman keeps promising what clearly will never be delivered. ("Sigh — if only we had met under different circumstances . . . ") Each woman receives ego strokes and neither is hurt or disappointed.

You will best understand the following suggestions for keeping romance alive if you are over a certain age or have stood in romance's magic, been broken, but still appreciate the glow. Courtly Lesbians understand that Romance is never permanent, but that our need for it is eternal.

Romantic Emanations to Cultivate

☆ Always arrive with a faerie token: a single flower, a bouquet of herbs, a sweet, or anything handmade.

☆ Hide another little gift or note for your beloved to find when you are gone.

☆ Create a surprise anniversary for a moment you have never forgotten.

☆ Arrange in every day a moment for the pure vacation of being with her, however brief.

☆ Try to live your lives in meetings and partings forever.

☆ Take the path of heart and emotion to sexual intimacy; do not depend on sex to lead you to the heart.

☆ Compliments. Compliments. Compliments. A day without compliments is a day without romance.

☆ Delete all mention of your own deficiencies.

☆ Do not complain about anything, large or small. Leave the room, or even the city, until you can behave like an attractive stranger.

☆ Regularly call her by a new endearment, and remember her favorites.

☆ Do not be dramatic. Dramatize your beloved.

☆ Write love notes to create lasting waves in the sea of attraction.

☆ Do not assume your beloved feels as romantic as you do, so take care to "set the scene."

☆ Do not, in fact, assume anything.

☆ Never change your perfume.

☆ Remember to kiss the downy hairs on the nape of her neck, the sensitive pulse of her wrist, and to gently blow warm love breaths into her ear.

☆ Never send an unsolicited photo. Ask her for one.

☆ Draw a small heart on her mirror with soap.

☆ Never provoke jealousy; everything is already fragile.

☆ Do not be mysterious, be private.

☆ Remember that charm is more potent than intellect.

☆ Remember that understanding is more potent than charm.

☆ Do not impose plans on your beloved when she wants to read or nap or enjoy the scenery.

☆ Be always ready to lay down your arms, not without a sense of wonder.

☆ Take all the above, notably yourself, lightly.

II.
Bedside
Manners:

Lesbian Sex Treats & Social Perils

A nd so we move from the playing fields of High Romance to those of High Touch. You have stormed passion's gate with a single rose, and now . . . . What follows is not a Lesbian sex manual, but a few suggestions for inner hospitality. It is sometimes difficult to remain calm discussing Lesbian sex since to society Lesbianism is both exotic darling and profound terror combined. This is a lot of fallout for ordinary Lesbians to bear. Relax, everyone. Let us forgive any schizoid hysteria over Lesbian sex (over *all* sex), and wish everybody the Big Easy where kisses run free. To us, sex is but one of the forms of Lesbian communication, another social skill making earthtime especially sweet. Lesbians even, it is said, find in sex a metaphysical chalice, one of the cups of wisdom life offers her devotees. Much of the time, however, Lesbian sex is nothing extraordinary, a way to breathe in life and pleasure as we breathe in air. The happy naturalism of Lesbian sexuality is that the initial physical responses are usually easy and harmonious, quite independent of Tab XY being able to rise, fit and stay in Tab XX — with XX being ultimately responsible for any resulting birth, death, pain and child support. Lesbian sex tends to be pure pleasure, and, unencumbered with male domination ideology, a passionate emotional exchange with lots of intimacy.

Lesbians shake their heads at the fact that one out of every two hetero marriages is a "sexual disaster area," according to Masters and Johnson. Shere Hite's latest study, *Women & Love: A Cultural Revolution in Progress*, found that 87 percent of the 4,500 women surveyed, regardless of sexual preference (11 percent identified as Lesbians), derived their greatest emotional fulfillment from other women. Thirty-four percent of the Lesbians over forty had left heterosexual marriage for woman love; is this the "Cultural Revolution in Progress" of the subtitle? Seventy-six percent of Lesbians rated their sex lives as "good," but the majority of heterosexual women were angry and hurt by the male tendency to "withhold and distance." Male commentators sputtered and split percentage hairs, but the resounding message of heterosexual women's sexual disappointment is repeated in survey after survey.

An Ann Landers poll of 90,000 women asked, "Would you be content to be held closer and treated tenderly and forget about *the act?*" A resounding 72 percent voted to nip the act and lengthen the intimacy. Ann, after thirty years in the wisdom-dispensing business, allowed she was "not surprised." She added, "There are many women out there who are so dissatisfied with their sex lives that they'd just as soon not be bothered with it." Wham, bam, thank you, Ann. A "Dear Abby" poll revealed that even "happily" married women are dissatisfied with their men. Surveys by *Redbook, Women's Day, New Woman, Glamour,* and *Cosmopolitan* reveal the same dreary theme. It has always been agreed among the Ladies that heterosexual men are among our best recruiters. If heterosexual men who truly love women don't somehow get in touch, well, as Aretha sings, "Sisters are doing it for themselves . . . . "

A woman instinctively and intuitively knows how to pleasure another woman, having her own body and its sweet arousals as loving teacher. Her guiding touch and motion naturally express her own special preferences and rhythms; she is simply doing as she would be done by — or utterly undone, as the case may be. We have empathy as ecstasy: "Here?" "Ahhh, here." "And here . . . " "Yes, there." Lesbian sex is unique not so much for its libidinal prepositions, but for being richly blended rather than genitally focused. Lesbians dance all colors of the rainbow, not just one end. Besides fingers, tongues, breasts, honey baskets, hair, bellies, and on and on, our taste for High Romance also eroticizes everything with sweet talk and music. Then we bring on imaginative indulgences like finger food, feathers, and fancy dress, from leather to old lace. Women, as the long distance dancers of sex, have delicious staying power together and can sustain what Lady Clitoressa awesomely calls "a kinetic stillpoint" for which orgasm is only the beginning.

The Seduction Dinner

Eating manners, gusto and special tastes often reflect sexual style, so the Ladies say it is well to dine with a prospective lover. Indeed, some Lesbian sex practices demand a multi-vitamin body, so eating around is an especially good prelude. The best seduction dinner is one you fix yourself because you can customize the food and setting to her pleasure, and the home-grown and handmade emanates personal aura. "I know a quiet little place" may involve a noisy little bus ride. Best to be a few steps from the bedroom as desire rises.

The only rule for a seduction dinner, at home or out, is that you consider it simply a nourishing *beau geste* in the whole seductive adventure, not necessarily "the" night. This lowers the anxiety level enormously. The romantic bistro dinner in the Lesbian memoirs, *ELSA, I Come with My Songs* by Elsa Gidlow, illustrates how full courses of intimacy set with subtle invitations may nourish another night's crescendo. Never assume the lady will stay that night, though planning and preparing for this event is part of the fun. The seduction dinner is a moment to exhibit the intimate plumage of home and hearth: your attentive hospitality, good taste, or even your first unified set of china. Be patient; love is a moveable feast. The lady may need to reflect on the lay of the land before she settles in, or be so nervous she prefers to make love together for the first time in her own bed, or be worried about feeding the cats. After all, the invitation was for dinner, not for a slumber party.

Greet her with a sisterly hug. Maintain eye, not thigh, contact. Say grace like a spiritual person, if only to yourself and Saint Vivant. Toast her, not "us" (too blatant). Be sure to have flowers and give her a special one to take home, whether morning or evening. Candles are a must; linen napery is preferred. Spare us the colored sex-signal bandanna napkins, as again confusing and somehow relentless. Oysters may also be a case of trying too hard, and artichokes push the metaphor too, but if you know she loves them . . . Just be sure to find out what she hates. Many Lesbians are purists about not consuming meat or alcohol, so you may have to make a choice between your habits and her. If tempted to drink too much at dinner, remember there is an excellent champagne for brunch. You have not gone to all this work to be, or to deal with, a sloppy drunk. Who ever said being a hedonist was easy?

A good menu choice is high protein, perhaps what was once called simple *nouvelle cuisine*, with its petite portions (everyone is aflutter) of ultra-fresh natural foods arranged artfully on the plate. Think circles. Nouvelle cuisine is good for its simple finesse, visual artistry, and, well — nakedness. No heavy, masking sauces of Mixmaster-induced combinations to confuse the senses. For at least this night, if corporations made it, don't serve it. Prepare instead something like hearts of palm, circlets of scallions, tiny shrimp or braised endive which may be tactually savored, since Lesbians *love* finger food. Such morsels may be fed to one another if things have reached that pitch. Sometimes salads are avoided because lettuce leaves are reputed to be anaphrodisiac. Aphrodite threw herself on a bed of lettuce to cool her ardors. Since not serving salads in places like California is, however, almost a breach of etiquette, one of the Ladies designed a special salad for seduction dinners. Yes, you can eat it with your fingers. The "trick," as they gaily say in *Cosmo*, is in using romaine lettuce "boats."

Sylvia's Seduction Salad

Wash a head of romaine and dry each leaf well with a napkin. Toast a piece of bread, stroke it gently with garlic, cut the toast crisscross into four diamonds, and place these in a salad bowl. Arrange the leaves of romaine over the toast. Soft-boil two eggs, and spread them over the leaves. Mix three tablespoons of light olive oil, three of lemon juice, and some pepper and pour this in. Sprinkle grated parmesan cheese over the top with roasted sesame seeds.

When you retire to the couch for coffees and faerie pudding, then, and only then, consider whether you want to "make the move." You may wish to simply angle for another evening of anticipation or an invitation to dinner at her home. If there is anything more exciting than one seduction dinner, it is two. If the time seems right, it is proper for the host to make the move. "I wish you didn't ever have to leave tonight." This puts nobody on the spot, but gets the point across. Remember, you can seduce no one who doesn't want to be; both of you decide how much energy you want to exchange. Sharing a beautiful dinner and conversation is a high holy and sensuous act which can be fulfilling in and of itself, but sweet dreams . . .

The First Time, or A Long Undressing

With each new woman, it is always the first time. You are likely to feel flustered, so futures may be hotter, but there is nothing like the dawning of carnival knowledge. Some Lesbians, in fact, known in the life as "curious," major solely in first times. Theirs are really two times, the first and the last.

"Firsts" require sensitivity and care to minimize gawkiness. Natural awkwardness and shyness, however, are as charming as a Natalie Barney blush. These, in fact, are a must in the special erotica of "newness," so never appear "pro." Fumbling around with the buttons is not exactly a turn-off. Be reassured that some women are pre-orgasmic at first; this means you have a long beginning. Veteran planners, however, do well during amateur hour because they have thought of the little things that relax a guest lover. Lady Clitoressa designed her bedroom as "a church for two." Install a lighting system bright enough to see where the furniture is, but which can be dimmed for first-night delicacy. The phone is turned off, the answering machine down. A candle in glass to disperse the flame should be immediately accessible, as well as a choice of something to drink. A gardenia at the bedside is redolent, but any fragrant flower is memorable.

Some *amours* flame quickly. Rolling around on the floor curtails the pre-nuptial chit-chat. Often the pyrotechnics come later. The move is made, accepted. Then comes the rather bashful, but exquisite, "settling in." Just going through the motions of host like, "These are the fresh towels," besides being *de rigueur*, help diffuse nervousness. Finally, "This is the bed, these are my arms . . . " If extreme modesty is the wear, you will get signals. Shame may be a bourgeois notion, but privacy is aristocratic. Honor it. Offer her the bathroom first. Note any closed door and respect it. Get undressed quickly yourself and turn down the bed, so when she comes out things are moving along. You might go in the bathroom or somewhere so she can undress and get into bed. Bring the drinks, light the candle . . . and we leave you on the plains of pubis, under a blessed moon, moving easily into the song of the river's body . . .

The Morning After

After waking your lover with a kiss and a hug and doing whatever else makes your souls purr, it is back to everyday Lesbian etiquette, exact manners depending on whether you want a repeat performance. If not, offer her coffee and a croissant, telling her you have to be out and about. Bustle unromantically, but not rudely. You may mention that you have so much work to do you'll be busy the next six months, but never be churlish. You always owe true politeness to any woman whose affections you have encouraged and won. Naturally you have combined integrity with your romantic glamour, so you have nothing to confess to her, like your special lover of three years is due home imminently.

If you found the experience glorious, you may wish to begin a liaison, so plan accordingly. Always have an extra robe or sleep coat so you can both loll around and have brunch. The last thing you want her to do is get dressed. Used clothing stores have racks of virtually new designer robes, so you can get a couple of classy styles for a song. One size nearly fits all, you rogue. Have food for brunch or offer to take her out. It is unforgivable to be out of coffee, cream, tea, or juice. Over brunch, set up the next date, or you will worry that all has been a beautiful fantasy. The next day it is courtly to send one another loving thank-you notes to link love-making to love. If you are unpracticed at *billets doux*, a simple "Thank you for *everything*" is allusive, if not effusive. A sprig of lavender or "rosemary for remembrance" helps lean prose. Writing paper with your engraved monogram does too. A small investment in engraved stationery will probably last you the rest of your love life. Never have your monogram merely printed offset, without texture. Lesbians have sensitive fingertips.

Exotic Persuasions
& Adventurous Amours

Lesbians are holistic practitioners of sex, but there are specialties, even fads, like s & m. Sometimes it is embarrassing to tell your lover, new or old, you want to park in a car and make out like a bandit or to hit the lingerie departments with her to fool around in the dressing room. It can be a delicate matter to bring up that you fantasize licking peach mousse from her you-know, like to be spanked, or want her to pretend she is a lustful nun.

Begin by letting her know you are interested in her fantasies and would like to participate. Rarely can a proposal be so repulsive and immoral (to you) that it would harm the total relationship. If so, don't do it. We all have our snake pits of taboo. Let her know you still love her madly, but not that particular fantasy. Nothing is really so terrible, unless it is coercive. A fantasy is just a fantasy. Most of us have "core" fantasies going back to childhood. Some can be downright fun, acted out. For example, anything messy, from body finger-painting to mud-wrestling, usually is. A great turn-on to one woman, however, may be anti-erotic to another — being peed on, for example. If one woman is hot while the other is disgusted, find a mutually pleasurable kink. These are legion and can be a banquet of delights. For one thing, boredom does not set in. Doing outrageous things with your lover also can mean great intimacy and trust, creating another bond. Many taboos are in fact acted out only with a special lover. Anal sex and using dildoes, like most things on the lube circuit, or bondage, or popping the controversial drug "ecstasy," are not what you usually do with just anybody on the first night.

The use of dildoes once presented a splendid question of propriety among Lesbians. Held for years to be politically incorrect by feminists as the embodiment of intrusive maleness, dildoes have slipped from the taboo charts, approaching Lesbian mainstream. Gigantic, rigid dildoes are, of course, the absurdly narcissistic staple of male porno. Recently, however, dildoes are being made with quality silicon, including double dildoes. Some, almost ritual

46

objects, are now exquisitely sculpted into statues of diving women. They are soft and bouncy, and they actually fit if you get them at a women's mail order sex-toy shop like Good Vibrations or Eve's Garden.* Some Lesbians find dildoes as amusing as the organ itself and bob them about in madcap ways. The Ladies wonder, is the dildoe a penis substitute, or is it the other way around? As a rule of (ahem) thumb, many Lesbians do not use dildoes or even an organic version like carrots, cukes or bananas, so go slow and build up to them. Vibrators are a bit more acceptable. It is always best to discuss erotic sex practices and sex toys with your lover first, preferably when you both are hot. As in all delicate situations, communication is the best lubrication.

S & M, Us & Them?

The Lesbian sexuality award for the best lucubration certainly goes to the forces of sadomasochism. Slap-happy is an acquired taste, one quite a few Lesbians have tasted, but few acquire, despite its large press and hetero *chic*. Most of the worldly women in Lady Clitoressa's Circle find the s & m concept rather stupefying, like slam-dancing. They hold disdain for s & m because s & m behavior is a *cliché*. Women of originality can rarely bear to become caricatures of patriarchal dominance/submission. Another aspect of s & m which is anti-erotic to many Lesbians is its sado-puritan side. Much of its "feeling" is based on terrible and unreal guilts. Moreover, burns, fissures and hepatitis do not make your body more interesting.

Lady Clitoressa herself, however, declares that s & m is one of the more valuable heresies in the Feminist Religion. Like all heresies, she says, it has a kernel of truth and important libertarian value. The s & m's, whom she calls "us & thems," deserve credit for exposing not only the presence but the pathology of dominance and submission in all of us. How often do we conduct our relationship conflicts in a verbal s & m theater of violence, never acknowledging that psychological pain can be as cruel as physical? S & m dramatically reveals to us that all relationships are based on elements besides love — and these are power and control.

S & m also underscores such cosmic truths as impermanence and interdependence. It dramatizes that all ego roles are really forms of "let's pretend," as when tonight's most carefully crafted "top" bottoms out in daylight or the "switch hitter" acknowledges her persona is dynamic, not static. Further, the identity of the seemingly imperial top is entirely dependent on a partnership model, on some-

---

* Send $1 each for the zesty catalogs of: Eve's Garden, 119 West 57th St., #1406, New York, NY 10019; Good Vibrations, 3942 22nd St., San Francisco, CA 94110.

one else's willingness to enact a contrasting role, and to hold up a validating mirror. Who is *really* in control? Each is in it together.

S & m brought more colors to Lesbian sexuality than just black and blue. Its proponents did much to introduce the pleasures of fetish and fantasy, of ritual, games and roles. Women, however, do not have to select the iconography of fascism for exciting sexual theater. For example, ritual "S & S," sex and spirituality, is among the loving, powerful alternatives described in later chapters. S & S is said to be "the favorite of Ladies who prefer lather to leather." S & m also brought our diversity in pain/pleasure thresholds to light. Let's face it, for some, it may be love at first bite. What is raw pain to you may be blissfully stimulating to a tiger cub of a Lesbian. It is a wisely erotic Lesbian who understands that the power of sensation turns and whirls like the yin/yang fish in different stages of passion and differently among individual awarenesses.

Finally, all of us, not just leather faeries, surely long for the deep release of entrusting ourselves to a body and will different from our own, just as we delight in the potency of our body and will arousing and shaping a lover's ecstasy. Perhaps the essential question to ask is: when is it foolhardy or exploiting to play with profound forces like our sensational limits — and when is it healing and transformative? Does our motivation come from the will to power or does it flow from the heart of love's energies? Is your higher self on top?

The Bisexual Swing

A less provocative, but still fascinating, heresy with infinite possibilities is bisexuality. Yes, many sorts of women and men have had and will have sex with self-defined Lesbians. This should not be a problem as long as there is no danger of AIDS transmission. Remember safe sex! The Ladies wish the inexact term "bisexual" did not exist except in the technical accuracy of a person having sex with a woman and a man at the same time. Each of the self-defined, and constantly redefining, six sexes (female and male gays/straights/bi's) may have sex in at least thirty-six combinations with each other. "Bisexual" seems a bit vague in our vari-sexual and multidimensional world. Bifriendly? There is the old chestnut that bisexual men are men who cannot admit to being gay and bisexual women are women embarrassed to be straight, but perhaps bisexuality is an experimental or transitional phase which is pleasantly long, even of life duration, for some people who will switch sexes in the next.

Bisexual trashing by gays comes about because bisexuality appears to give credence to homophobic belief that there is no such thing as a homosexual. Well, we Lesbians need not bother to refute that one. There is also the fear that bisexuals merrily taste our fruits, then when oppression to homosexuals rears its ugly head, the bisexuals will invoke their "heterosexual privilege" and deny us like Judases. In truth, bisexuals are just like the rest of us, some trustworthy, some not. Many Lesbians still want bisexual women to make an either/or "final" choice. But is not the fundamental gay affirmation that everyone should be free to love whomever they wish?

What we might enjoy and learn from the bisexy drama in the vast arena of sexuality is that on-stage genital games only suggest a genre. For the real action, watch the out-of-bed scenes for loyalty, authenticity and evolution. Is the character's "outercourse" one of feminist values (power with/within) or masculinist (power over)? When and why is one character's style receptively feminine and when energetically masculine? Is the actor the creator of her own script; are her love songs honest? Bisexuality is a good question to ponder just when you think you've got everything figured out.

Celibacy

This may well bring us to what Lesbians respect as one of the most exotic (and het-tabooed) sexual forms of relating to people: celibacy. Celibacy is the thoughtful, thoroughly considered affirmation and nurturance of oneself by directing sexual energy into alternative circuits. It is not an accidental state of unwilling chastity. Mystics have long understood that sexual energy can be a marvelous, powerful form of spiritual energy. Celibacy can "play" one's sexual stream into heart-consciousness and thereby unite us with cosmic wholeness. We sometimes forget that our sexual tides may be routed inward (innercourse?) to reach communication with one's higher self. Why adopt the "requirement" that sex should always be directed outward in orgasm, whether in masturbation or with another person?

Lesbians often take vows of celibacy to be able to focus high creative energy on their art, profession, or studies. We do this sometimes without even thinking about it. We may need celibacy to root ourselves before entering into an important relationship with another woman's power and realities, or to build a loving relationship with ourselves. We may need to heal from incest or rape. We may simply wish to explore how to build another kind of loving relationship which is not buffeted by the turbulent winds of sex. There are, after all, other avenues to love and intimacy than genital and orgasmic sex. Sharing quality time and deep emotion, affinity to a cause, or partnership in an important joint venture can all be blessed with affection and tenderness, *and* highly tuned eroticism. We can, for example, choose to relate in a visual, imaginative or astral level with another woman. This is not the same as genital sex, but it is not less. All of us must be celibate at some times in our lives and must always be celibate with some people (your best friend's gorgeous lover, your boss, your spiritual teacher). It is wise to skillfully learn to embrace celibacy when appropriate. She will treat you well.

Lesbians often find celibacy useful after a hard break-up. We can step back and explore the dynamic of change, what went wrong, what to improve; we can take time to grieve and let go. Running immediately into someone else's arms may doom you to repeat the same old pattern; you are not healed and changed, but diverted.

A period of considered celibacy may last months, years or a lifetime — as long as it is useful and strengthening. Celibacy, above all, is not a punishment or penitence. Women are truly peaceful with their celibacy or they end the practice. Nor is celibacy asexual. Many a celibate leads a merry sex life with herself and a sensuous one with the world. Making love to one's self, says Lady Clitoressa, is one of the great yogas: it delights and centers without the blurring complications. It is also nice to discover how amazingly erotic the whole flowering world is — no genital fix required.

Here are a few tips from the Celibacy Liberation Front if you want to try practicing celibacy:

1) Simply watch your sexual energy and don't expect it to suddenly disappear. Don't argue with or deny this old friend. It is, in any event, too powerful a force to resist, so just wave to it with a smile as it passes.

2) And it does pass, flowing in and out like the tides. Feel how interesting it is to ride it out, especially if you can "run" the energy into a creative channel.

3) Try to avoid sexual stimulation, very difficult in a culture where sex is blared from the rooftops.

4) Do relaxation exercises like deep breathing, yoga and meditation.

5) Express a great deal of non-fixated affection toward all beings: cats, plants, people you really like and ones you could like if you didn't judge everyone as a possible sex partner.

6) Don't tell anyone but your significant other(s) you have gone celibate; most people are rather disruptive over celibacy. Let them guess why you look so free and calmly energized.

7) Diet considerations: meat, onions, garlic and all the spicy foods stimulate sexual energy; so do caffeine and nicotine.

8) Exercise as much as you can doing the physically active things

you love. Certain yoga postures and breathing exercises are designed to run sexual energy in delicious alternative ways.

9) Remember celibacy is like jogging; you don't have to do it *every* day.

The great irony of celibacy is that Lesbians who forthrightly adopt a celibate period can become even more desirable to others. The wild thing about celibacy is you can do it with many people at once. One of the most arousing of bookazines is the cool, uncluttered sex talk and poetry of *The Celibate Woman*★, subscribed to by tantrics and celibates alike. While celibates may inspire the old "forbidden fruit" allure, their attractiveness is often in their display of a wonderful inner light of self-worth. Here is someone non-needy, with few obsessive/possessive ways of relating. In an era when sex, not religion, is the opiate (and amphetamine) of the people, those who have kicked such addiction are free to go about their lives. Notice celibates are often super-achievers: entrepreneurs, black belts, politicos, artists. They are building something meaningful while those of us on sexual automatic pilot can barely get home to feed the cats. Because a sexual love is one of the most common, immediate and lovely forms of excitement, we tend to think sex is essential to life. "What is essential to life," says Lady Clitoressa, "is excitement herself."

Welcome to the Pleasure Dome

Once upon a time, around a faerie fire with the spiced cider flowing, some members of Lady Clitoressa's Circle were emboldened to relate their favorite off-beat sexual pleasures. (Perhaps most Lesbian pleasures are "off-beat," since we never rely on the rote missionary position, a.k.a. "the squashed bug.") A survey in *Lesbian Passion* by Lesbian sex therapist Joann Loulan★★ found that even lesbian oral sex, another male porno staple, is far from universal. Lesbians have an open menu, from body rubbing (that's *tribadism* and *frottage* if you like a French zing) to oral delights and finger frolics all around. We enjoy the entire organ of warm skin, a moving universe of lovetides to explore.

★ *The Celibate Woman*, 1982-1988, $4 per issue. All eight issues are still in print. Order from: 3306 Ross Place, NW, Washington, DC 20008.

★★ Joann Loulan is the merry minstrel of Lesbian advice and research. her books, *Lesbian Passion* (1987) and *Lesbian Sex* (1984), are great and her performances are show-stoppers of hilarity and hot sex talk. Her tapes are available from Loulan Productions, 1450 6th St., Berkeley, CA 94710.

Here is a brief menu of the Ladies' special entrees before they breathlessly detail the recipes. Meet Constance and Scarlett first because they are leading exponents of the two great contrasting schools of Lesbiana which we will discuss later, Monogamy and Pluralism. Seemingly dignified Constance may be a sexual macrobiotic when it comes to reserving herself for one partner, but in bed she is Queen of Fantasies for her lover, a Scheherazade of tales to enact and roles to play from silk neckties to satin panties. Perhaps variety is her spice of life after all. Scarlett, the merry rover, has a wicked penchant for public sex, not the intrusive exhibitionist variety, but "hide & seek" games under the very nose of the patriarchy. Zenia, with the luminous eyes (and fingers) of a *yogini*, loves to practice highly focused ritual sex to consciously reach the stillpoint where flesh and spirit coalesce, where the heat of body pulse throbs to Light. Concha pours the water of life into her poetic lovemaking, giving sensuous showers and fragrant baths by candlelight, foot washing massages, every toe an organ. And meet Kemble, the seasoned, seagoing lover every woman would want as her first, whose "deep beyond deep" kisses all say, "May the flow be with you."

Are you ready for this? "No," says Lady Clitoressa, "not until we talk about safe sex." Uh-oh.

A Pause for Safe Sex

Lady Clitoressa, known for her own eighty-year-old staying power, does not intend to lose any Lesbian to AIDS ignorance. She is right. Careless blood or semen contact with an AIDS carrier, and you may be off to eternity. Gratefully, the Lesbian community has been spared contagion since our usual sex practices are low risk. Lesbian sex acts *per se* rarely include the commingling of bloods or contaminated needles, and none of them involve semen. Religious fundamentalists who rave that AIDS is an angry god's punishment for sinners should logically conclude their god then favors Lesbian sex practices as his most holy. In the thousands of reported AIDS cases in the United States, there are only a few unclear, remotely possible, instances where woman-to-woman AIDS transmission may have occurred. As a world-wide epidemic, AIDS is largely a heterosexual disease. In the United States, however, intravenous drug users and gay men are the hardest hit because of high-risk behavior. It is not who you are, but what you *do* that invites AIDS. Even the blessed state of Lesbianism does not confer immortality if you put yourself in high-risk situations.

Sex for women has, of course, never been "safe," shadowed as it is by vulnerability and death: pregnancy dangers, abortion, rape, incest, venereal disease, even the awesome death of ego, of control. AIDS has deepened the light irrevocably. The gay community is being shaken to its spiritual roots, which are going deeper to learn from the dark. Never has there been such a great planting of compassion, healing and unity among gay people. Once any beloved person dies, we understand the lover now in our arms is dying, even in passion, as we ourselves are. What can we do but make love to life more profoundly?

One way is choosing Lesbian "smart sex" loving for you and yours. (Again, *when* has sex for Lesbians ever been "safe"?) AIDS, like other sexually transmitted diseases, "STD's," can be curtailed using simple guidelines. If only cancer, a killer so virulent in Lesbians, could be dealt with as perfunctorily. In the United States, about ten times as many women die of breast cancer as do all people of AIDS. We do know AIDS is caused by an equal opportunity virus, one totally amoral, like all viruses. This one is named "HIV," human immunodeficiency virus. It attacks and destroys our immune system so that the body is completely vulnerable to a variety of life-threatening illnesses. HIV's proven highway of invasion is infected semen or infected blood, which must enter into another's bloodstream to kill. It is the semen connection which puts Lesbians at such low risk. A high concentration of HIV is possible in sperm, and the speed at which sperm can be released into a partner tends to preserve HIV, which is extremely fragile outside the body. Lesbians who may have occasional sex with men must therefore be queens of condom sense. No condom, no cum, fellas. Unprotected penis/vagina, penis/anus sex can transit AIDS. Period.

Intelligent and loving gay men have overwhelmingly adopted smart-sex practices, such as condom use, in one of the most unparalleled, self-monitored health programs a community ever embraced. "It's an upheaval, yet a renaissance of sorts. We're moving from hyper-sex to safe sex and caring," said one gay man. Gay males are naturally high-risk due to anal sex practices where both semen and blood exchanges may be involved, and also due to the widespread opportunity for multiple partners within gay male culture. Because of smart-sex practices, however, AIDS incidence in San Francisco would be on the decline among gay men as a class were it not for AIDS' often lengthy asymptomatic incubation period of several years. Smart sex is preventing new transmission, but gay men are becoming symptomatic from HIV received years past, before we knew how AIDS spread.

What about exclusively woman-to-woman AIDS transmission? While government AIDS statisticians publish data on studies on the varieties of gay male sex practices, women are presumed totally heterosexual in tabulations, so there are no officially published figures on Lesbian AIDS. What? Subsidize the delicious technicalities of woman-to-woman sex in government documents for all to read? Cum on. Claiming our own rights to sexual representation, the Lesbian population must conclude for itself that blood, the other proven avenue for transmission besides semen, remains our main AIDS link. Lesbians, therefore, who are not sure they themselves or their woman partner is safe, should prevent any commingling of their bloods via needles, and any exchange of blood via wounds or minor lesions anywhere, even the tiniest tearing of delicate tissue linings in mouth, vagina or anus; they should also be careful of menses transmission. One reported case of woman-to-woman AIDS transmission, an intravenous drug user and her non-user lover, may have involved infected blood exchange via vaginal bleeding caused by "traumatic" sexual activity and/or menses contact. ("Traumatic" in medical lingo is abrasions, cuts, wounds — anything more acute than a nail scratch.) Perhaps there was s & m sex? Details are sketchy, with bisexual activity also a theme in the unsolved mystery.

What to do? Clearly, if you are involved with any intravenous drug using or users, prevent the conscious or oblivious sharing of needles and paraphernalia. Sterilize all dope works with bleach. Flush the needle out twice by drawing bleach into the syringe to fill it, and shoot the bleach into the sink. Then rinse the syringe by filling it with water twice and shooting that out. "Death hits" with needles were also made by medical blood transfusions after AIDS was discovered in 1979. Since March of 1985, all blood is screened, so question transfusion history between 1979 and March of 1985. In the fall of 1985, sperm banks also began to screen donors. Prospective Lesbian mothers must insist on similar screening of any donor for their own health and that of their child.

A first step, obviously, is to review your own history for the past five or more years and then to find out if your lover is at risk. Because AIDS may incubate asymptomatically for an average of five years, gird your loins for a "meaningful conversation" to discuss recent histories involving blood transfusion, alternative insemination, male lovers, and needle users (gulp). Consider general health history too. Like any disease, AIDS most easily makes inroads when the body's immune system is already stressed by poor nutrition, drugs and alcohol, lack of rest, other infections, or emotional travail. Studies show that some people repeatedly exposed to HIV in vagina/penis sex did not get AIDS. If this candid, but delicate, little trip down memory lane does not totally exhaust you both, you may each have found your life's companion.

If either of you still does not quite have the requisite peace of mind for sex, but your desire is worth any test love can devise, take the AIDS antibody test. This test is able to detect only that your body has for some reason produced special HIV antibodies — and produced them previous to the last six months. So, if you take the antibody test and get negative results, practice safe sex for six months, then re-take the test to carry you up to the present. Or, practice safe sex six months before you take the test in the first place. Make sure the test is totally confidential *and* anonymous, since discrimination abuses have occurred with unauthorized distribution of positive results. The ELISA, or AIDS antibody test, is notorious for "false positives," especially in women, so be prepared to take the more accurate but complex Western blot as a follow-up test. Call your public health department or AIDS organization for a safe place to be tested.★

Finally, if you have any reason to know or suspect that you or your lover may be at risk from the past AND if either of you presently has a visible or even suspected wound or sore anywhere or is menstruating, ask to use "latex barriers" during sexual contact. Use them if you want to ask only one safe-sex question of a stranger, not take her ten-year biography — and remember people lie. If none of the above, try latex, anyway, for a great erotic diversion in your usual sex play. There's never any harm in "knowing how" to do a little latex lovin'. You'll be surprised how some quality of the material can sensationalize and smooth sex in a whole new way. Latex doesn't necessarily diminish elemental, hot sex any more than a bed does, and it can make some things more comfortable and amusing.

Handy latex barriers are "dental dams," "finger cots," latex gloves and condoms. Condoms are great for sex toys like dildoes. You don't have to jump up and wash toys between users or orifices; just peel off one condom, put on another and carry on. "Dental dams" are five-inch latex squares (get the largest ones) that come in silly colors and flavors as well as "regular" dusty grey. Use these capes over any orifice to prevent actual contact, while inviting sexy tongue and finger sensations. Dams also keep pubic hair out of your mouth and nose. A tip of the clit to the Lesbian dentist who invented a pleasant use for the damn things; they are manufactured to isolate teeth during torturous dental sessions. In sex play, it may take a little practice to keep dams in place, and you have to remember in the heat

---

★ Or, call the twenty-four hour national AIDS hotline, 1-800-342-7504.

of passion which side went where, so you can even mark them. Some Lesbians like clear plastic wrap better than dams. "Finger cots," little condomettes or "gloves" for just one finger, have also moved from the doctor's office to rosier fields. Use these with water-based lubrication jellies to make any penetration a sleek, satiny anointment of passion. The recipient feels no nail or skin edges and her sometimes acidic love juices can't sting the minor cuts a partner's fingers are heir to. Thin latex gloves seem a bit overdressed for most occasions, although love is a many-fingered thing. You can even get them in black now. It is amazing how easily you can forget you are wearing these ultra-thin gloves, how easily they convey a sense of warmth and wetness. Latex barriers are handy to know about because they can also protect Lesbians from other STD's (aaargh) like herpes, chlamydia, vaginitis.

Above — or perhaps below — all, use latex protection for anything you do in your lover's sweet ass, from "rimming" to "finger waving" to "fisting." Rimming is stimulating her wildly sensitive nerve endings at anal entry with your tongue. A dental dam natural. The intestinal tissue within is beautifully designed for nutrient absorption, so there are myriads of tiny blood cells very close to the surface. These can be easily broken by finger penetration, affording possible blood to blood contact if the finger has a small nick. So roll on a cot. Lesbian recipients of anal sex from a penis should remember that sperm can be absorbed by intestinal walls, with lining only one cell thick. Condom required, not optional. Latex gloves are an absolute essential for "fisting," the rather uncommon predilection for putting one's entire hand into a lover's anus, creating unusual pressure on the tissue since this area is not designed with the elasticity of the vagina. Whatever variation, remember the lower intestine is, for good reason, your teeming Microbe City. So cots or gloves should, as a matter of course, always be used, then thrown away. Thus, you won't pass along hepatitis, venereal disease, or parasites — problems for the adventurous long before AIDS.

Dental dams, finger cots and gloves are cheap and easily available in quantity from surgical supply companies listed in the *Yellow Pages*. No salesperson has *ever* been known to ask, "WHAT are you using them for?"

"Sex has always been a problem, but so has the weather," said Lady Clitoressa to move things along. "If space-age latex provides any resilient port in a storm, then put some in the little spice box by my bed."

III.
Back to the Pleasure Dome

We can now return to relax in the cozy scene around the fire, open to anything, even safe sex. What could be safer sex than merry sex talk? Don't ask me, however, if decorated condom balloons languidly rose at certain revelations, who discreetly caressed herself during the discussion, and who enjoyed what with whom afterwards . . . Here the names have been changed to honor the guiltless.

Constance: Tickled by the Wand of Fantasy

My love and I laugh that we are into "oral sex with a passion," the way we often like to stage hot-scripted dramas around our love-making. We discovered that sex, like food or almost anything inherently powerful, can be exciting theater in nice contrast to simple, repetitive ritual. We both used to fantasize separately, and still do, but being able to "flesh out" my stories or even verbalize them with my woman is very hot and intimate, and I like the freedom to play like a kid again. Mutual make-believe, with maybe a few improvised props or clothes, also offers more variety than solo fantasy. Our private theater reminds me that many of the roles people choose or just accept in society are so much "dress-up" too. Too bad the mutual make-believe out in the world has so little sensuality to beautify and lighten the performance.

"Chance meeting" is one of our favorite plays to re-enact because it harkens back to new sex in its mystery and possibility. A Lesbian declaration of passion to an unknown woman is always an exhilarating risk and adventure. Sometimes we use real places where we "meet"; sometimes we create everything from our bed at home. Depending on mood, our meeting and courting scene runs from idyllic (a spring wildflower hike, a rustic bed-and-breakfast inn) to a place which is supportive or suggestive (a Lesbian festival, strip show, or gym) to challenging, dangerous and forbidden (a Mormon conference, a two-week jail stay, the Planet-of-Try-Anything-Once). In "Jailhouse Romance," for example, a hot, shy virgin learns how to do her time easy from a hot, foxy Lesberado whose voyeuristic buddies keep watch for guards. Playing the "Lesbian Guard" role is a variation. The jail scenario was embroidered from the intensely marvelous yet hellish short jail terms one of us served for peace activism. We tried some other "theater of violence" scenarios, but they don't usually pan out erotically. I guess our only s & m accoutrements are a wild collection of silk ties we use for bondage and some sexy Mardi Gras masks which seem to be especially hot in hotel rooms we sometimes rent for the weekend.

We do a hundred variations of my core fantasy. I open my oh-so-proper, corporate office door to a bold woman with wicked, laughing eyes. She locks the door behind her, asks me to tell the switchboard to hold all calls, then rolls my business card around her finger as she slowly comes toward me, shaping her mouth into a kiss which begins to caress my whole body. I always play a shocked, utterly amenable, me. My love may play the woman as a tycoon; as a new, impossibly ardent lover; as a hooker — we negotiate and compare notes between her entrepreneurship and my "kept" corporate ways. In yet another variation, she arrives in my office as a Witch I once met at a sensual Pagan ritual; another time she is a stomping union organizer. My love also has a core fantasy we play for her, referred to fondly as the "course in miracles," which only she could explain to you.

We like to call each other at our offices and make absolutely outrageous sexual proposals. We tell each other what we want when we get home, and what we want the other to do to get ready. If the recipient of the call can be overheard in the office, she lets out a long, cool string of "yeses," and tries to look calm. We get some of our inspiration from erotic books, films and videos, and many from subtle, everyday provocations and possibilities. (The masseuse you wish would whisper softly, "How about a deep vaginal massage to really relax you?") If something works, we add it to our repertoire for a while. Trying on wanton ideas like one dons clothes can be a revelation of amazing and humorous sex. Once you accept that sex is as mental as it is genital, you can kiss all kinds of sexy "unreality" into juicy existence. Don't be shy. Hey, come to think of it, that's one of my favorite roles . . . .

Scarlett: Between the Sheets of the World

I've always enjoyed expressing romantic and sensual feelings in public with a lover, being in the street scene of love with crowds of people around. Privacy and closed doors have their essential place in romance, of course, but my passion sometimes likes to jump its banks to flow with the daily lifestream. I like to watch all kinds of other people being lovers too; they remind me it is a flowering world. Since the flowering of Lesbian passion is still an establishment taboo, I love to subtly arouse a lover while keeping everyone else fairly oblivious to the hot game we are playing in public — sort of having my cake and eating it too.

Remember the rousing sentiment of the Beatles' jolly song, "Why Don't We Do It in the Road?" So far my style is probably that of the earlier British artist, the great actor and wit Mrs. Patrick Campbell: do anything you please, just don't frighten the horses. I extend her consideration to any being who by sheer chance happens to be present when two women's sexual energy is flowing, admittedly pretty racy stuff. Whipping orgasmic sensuality into a frenzy forces others to become an audience without their consent. This is bullying exhibitionism. One needs to be a dancer or theatrical genius to actually involve an audience in any hard-core sexual shenanigans. But it is great fun and a special skill to sensually stoke and catch each other's woman-heat under the very pecker of an unsuspecting phallocracy. If my lover and I do allow our desire to become so insistent that it must take blushingly blatant form, we find some private hideaway to take the edge off, or we make a warm, anticipatory trip home, for which this was a great prelude.

I start small, especially if the other woman is a bit shy, like putting my hand under her thigh in a darkened theater. A church pew is another fine place to do this. "Active" hand holding in a theater is unobtrusive, but is a great fuse of suggestibility, rebounding with squeezes and explorations. My arm around her theater chair, or any chair, reminds her of my expansive wishes, but is somewhat discreet. It is fun to flirt a lover with compliments at a public event, especially when it's safe for the words to be overheard by other women. As she warms to them, I begin saying downright sexy things to her privately. The more formal or serious the occasion, the sexier the comment sounds in contrast. Spacious restaurants are my favorite place for sexual interludes. Only the waiter may know what is going on — and waiters often welcome the diversion. We have, after all, rented the table and the service to free us for total absorption and pleasure. We politely, albeit lingeringly, feed each other tastes of each order. After some subtle touching of hands and deep looks, I take off a shoe and caress her gently with my foot under the table. This is one time when long, full skirts are a blessing for bare, warm contact. Booths conceal the action best; their benches afford good leverage too. I myself have been toed almost to orgasm; then we went into the restroom for the *chef d'oeuvre*. No one usually has the wildest dream that we, with such impeccable manners, would do such a thing. All it takes is a little intrigue. Women's bars are, of course, more appropriate for bold, open moves, especially if you like other women watching.

I also like to park and make out. As a teenager with guys, I was very concerned about getting pregnant or a "reputation," so I learned the joy of wild woman "comes" to oral and digital sex. I still love the crazed fumbling around for sex in a hot, steamy car — now with the exotic danger of being discovered with a woman (gasp!). What if a woman cop sauntered up? One of the most satisfying places I ever made out with a woman was in the deserted garden of a historic California mission. We fondled each other to our knees, then our elbows. Our Lady smiled. I keep a soft blanket in my car because I never know when I may find the perfect outdoors place to make love. I always imagine the smell of sunshine on a woman's body as soon as I meet her.

Another of my favorite public sex adventures is to go shopping with a lover for sumptuous food to eat together in bed. We go to the fanciest produce store in the neighborhood and carefully select the most sensually cleavaged peaches, the plumpest papayas and juiciest berries. We carefully take measure of the dildoesque, slim and shining Japanese eggplants, the cukes and the zukes. Everyone else seems to be picking out produce on automatic pilot while we slowly tantalize each other with our baskets of delight. Lingerie shops are, of course, the browser's bazaar of *volupté* for hot Lesbian lovers. You don't know what excitement is until you have been eighty-sixed from a dressing room for a merry widow waltz. You'll probably hit the phone booths next, but only the ones painted halfway up, please. Accompany your lover to a manicurist and watch while her loving hands are unctuously massaged, her fingers spread wide, each one caressed before your eyes.

Society's restraints on any expressions of Lesbian sexuality heighten my rebellious excitement to engage in them all the more. What a benevolent world it would be if women could walk the streets arm in arm and could touch each other romantically in a cafe. Each of us has that world at our fingertips if we dare but create it. In my small way, carefully gauging any threat of male physical violence, I have decided to enjoy my sexual self out in the universe, home to *all* of us. When I began, I found I had overestimated the vigilance of the compulsory heterosexual censors and certainly their abuse power. Still, they exist. I can now dismiss a verbal assault with a half-smile and the fervent, silent compliment to myself, "I am glad *I* am not like that." I award us the Purple Heart every time I hold hands or kiss on my lady, and the eyes of the het-folks pop awake. It is good for them and their kids to see a love that dares. What more powerful way to diffuse the het terror? "Oh, my god, Mabel, I saw two women kissing in broad daylight and the sky didn't fall!"

In the face of actual physical danger, for me, discretion is definitely the better part of valor. My lover and I simply depart the field, as one of uncontrollable, destructive energy, an unnatural disaster in the making. I honestly say, "Take care," to the aggressor and put our backs to the wind. I have done essentially the same thing when I was threatened with a loss of my job for being seen romancing a woman on my own time. My heart is not for sale, nor is my breast its hermitage. The song of the Lesbian Boulevardiere is too fragrant on the wind.

Zenia: To Be Holy Sensual

I must tell all of you Ladies, who know what a holy roller I am now, that I was once your basic unchurched agnostic. When I became a Lesbian, I was so shocked at the depth of Judeo-Christianity's historic fear and persecution of homosexuals — and all women — that I became an atheist, almost as angry as that love-fearing Grand Poobah in the Sky. But love, "the limb loosener," as Sappho calls her, is also the anger loosener. Now, being initiated in the light-bearing as well as the vibrant darkness of woman-love rites, my erotic freedom fills me with authority and joy. Poor Poobah.

I am learning how women, in ritually opening vulvas, hearts and senses to each other, have the power to open realms of the sacred — realms not only far beyond mere churchianity, but realms infinitely beyond all perceived divisions, such as spirit/flesh. Making love with women, I have experienced flesh *as* spirit incarnate, our two unique, special physical bodies embraced and embracing the holy energy of love universal. My Ladies call this exchange "Interbeing," as distinct from the practice of Dualism. That every being is an embodied aspect of the Divine Spirit, a joyous confluence of spirit and flesh to be celebrated, is, of course, the essential, the ultimate heresy to worshipers of Dualism (Duelists?), the one Dualists most love to hate. Lesbian Interbeings say even Dualists are divine; they just don't remember that flesh too is a gift of the Goddess, that a woman giving birth is simply clothing spirit in matter.

For me, the world of non-dualistic spiritual sensuality opened with Diana, a woman with whom I was living in a passionate, tumultuous relationship. For an inexpensive getaway from our conflicts and arguments we were somehow directed to the sauna of a Hindu meditation retreat in the country. Here, once a month, it was "Women's Day." We arrived to find a frumpy, peeling pink, fifties motel. We dubiously went in for a five-dollar bill and our promise not to bring in drugs or glass bottles (as we had fully intended).

What to our wondering eyes should appear inside the motel but a honeycomb of sensuously appointed meditation and massage rooms and a flowering courtyard with pools and sauna. Along with cosmic graphics, statuary and earth-art of shells, crystals and cascading plants, this wonderful sanctuary held a startling spectrum of serenely nude women. Some were meditating or reading, being massaged, or eating. Some talked softly or chanted as Indian music rose and fell. Sunlight in the garden court caught the pool's iridescent drops in the curly deltas of the women. I raised my eyes from a jeweled *mons venus* to see a sign so beautifully calligraphed that it seemed to speak aloud: "In the Garden of the Senses, lies the Path to the Spirit."

The serenity and sensuality of the women, the sacred art and music were overwhelming as Diana and I went to a room to massage one another. I longed to diffract my ardor and feeling with the grass and the champagne left in the car. Instead, I began playing with my senses, alternately focusing, then dissolving them into calm, slowly rhythmic landscapes of reforming patterns, moving like the whorls of Diana's fingers on me. I relaxed into ecstasy, and understood for the first time why the word "ecstasy" literally means standing outside oneself; I was "beside myself," transcended. As the day unfolded, I felt deep communion, a knowledge that Diana, the women and I were the many faces of Our Mother of the Sensuous Spirit.

Home that night in bed, still feeling suspended in the "OM/womb" echoes of the day, we blessed each other's bodies as we would a chalice. Other nights, we began to learn how, with the absolute attention of prayer, we could make love so slowly that any ice left between us would melt before it ever hit the river. Orgasms would light the darkness to chart us on a swirling quest toward something I could only feel as an Interbeing of we two, of every woman's body and the Spirit. Months passed and old conflicts finally unraveled, yet, oddly enough, we realized we shouldn't live together as lovers. Our focus continues to be that of lifelong intimates, happily calling each other "Dharma Buns."

Gradually, when I was especially attentive and open with certain other lovers, I began to experience moments of intense awareness along with something which I thought of as marvelous psychedelic-flashback waves to Diana and to a whole womankind deity. My lover and I would clothe ourselves in sensuality, and I, secretly then, would sing a little song of reverence. We would experiment with lightly guiding our passion in a returning circuit through our bodies, sometimes by breathing consciously to slow down and to silence mind chatter, sometimes by contemplating the miracles of the physical details and the radiance of each other. I could often feel enfolded in a golden cape of unity, emotions and sensations in harmony. With this cape around me, I began to travel, sometimes with other beings; sometimes into a blue-black spaciousness lit with star-souls or with colors and designs; sometimes into simple, wordless understandings. I wondered if the "secret knowledge" of esoteric traditions was not any secret at all, but like this, infinitely more simple and more awesome than word-language can ever communicate.

Once I was out of bed, however, I pretty much blocked the integration of these creative experiences into my daily life or relationships. I wasn't sure how to process them, and I suspected I was being called into an openness and an acceptance of being which frightened me. I was afraid I could not handle such shifts in control, not to mention these flights of "non-ordinary" physical and psychic energy opened by live women, rather than by the man-made drugs which temporarily unified my fields.

I am still wondering, but I am not that afraid. More and more Lesbians are exploring the co-evolution of ardent, earthy woman-love with some form of visionary spiritual practice. This is natural since all spiritual paths coalesce in Love, and Lesbians interpenetrate the fiery altars of the Love Goddess with innate esoteric knowledge and devotion. We can easily pace our love-making, with an inborn rhythm to the slow moment arising in all its exquisite sensations, to feel our love-making as a meditation together. On the dramatic frontiers of unifying, androgynous Lesbian sexual energy — so existentially femme, so quintessentially butch — we experience each element, to fill each other and to become filled. As a Lesbian, I feel I inhabit the Great Circle which surrounds the embracing yin/yang fish of each gay person, which indeed surrounds all diversity in unity: femme/butch, receptive/energizing, self/other. In my androgyne lover's embrace, this Great Circle experientially becomes the circle of love-making, as each pulse undeniably welcomes us toward the Great Union.

I have heard Lesbian love adepts call holy sensuousness by many names: Awakening the Goddess, Mother Kundalini Rising, Shaking with Shakti, The Tantric Weave, The Eleventh Step, The Flowering Yoniverse. Whatever the tradition, those of us into "S &

65

S" (spirit and sex) seem to love ritual, adoration, pleasure, and the divine contemplation of joining with our beloved and the Universe. Because Lesbian sacred sex-play is with the Goddess, there are no god-all-mighty rules of service, no elaborate techniques or forms — unless, of course, these delight or comfort you. There is no aim; we are just exploring. We do whatever feels natural and lovely, trusting to the moment and each other.

After ritual bathing, we usually create some kind of simple altar together to invoke the fertile, renewing sensuousness of the earth, her eternal four elements and her changing seasons of being. On it, we set a single flower, fruit or natural object in wood or stone (to symbolize earth), along with a candle and incense (fire and air), and a liquid "communion" (to symbolize water). Any object can serve as an altar piece which helps us to pause to revere all life, revere our own higher powers, revere the miracle of our touch and unity in this moment. Altar pieces may include deity statues, Goddess and vaginal art, incense, sacred dildoes, bells, flutes and finger cymbals, even the wind chimes outdoors.

We may wear jewels or special garments to evoke the Goddess in each other and to invoke the Source Herself. Sometimes we rouge each other's nipples like temple priestesses. We dedicate a few beginning moments to peaceful meditation and to the blessing of one another and our love trust. Sometimes this is as short as a bow to "You, a Goddess, whose luster is like the morning sun." Or we may do a whole ceremony of offertory prayers, affirmations, call and response exchanges, dancing, chanting and humming, warmed with sweet touch and embrace. Sometimes I begin an erotic exchange by tracing the hundred names of the Goddess over and over my lover's body. I have used the crimson honey of her menstrual blood as ink. I may open each of her six lips with the juice of a fruit crescent from the altar. We also like full-body rubbing to trance state, awakening to laughter as pure as the angels'.

One practice we use to raise, run and blend our erotic and spiritual energies is called the "Rosary of the Chakras." The chakras are, as you know, the seven major "electric" energy-transforming areas of the body, which hold whirlpools of physical, emotional and mystic energy. Lesbians say their number may be infinite. "Chakra" is the Sanskrit word for "wheel." According to the holistic doctrine of the chakras, our bodily and spiritual well-being depends on our chakras being open, unblocked gateways to our streaming life-force energy, the energy known as *élan vital*, holy spirit, *prana*, *shakti*, *chi* or *da* in various traditions. The chakra wheel is the foundation of Indian and Chinese health care and spirituality as well as a major

66

focus in Cabalistic, Tantric and Taoist philosophies of well-being. Energy center opening is also the basis of Reichian therapy, upon which most of today's bodywork practices are based. In various teachings, each petaled pulsing chakra is arrayed with a luminous color aura, corresponding to a particular state of psychic awareness.

The first, the "root chakra," red in aura and relating to elemental survival instincts and material needs, is located at the base of the spine. If the chakras are an electrical circuit, the root chakra is our essential "ground." The base of the spine is also the seat of the great serpent goddess Kundalini, who slumbers there until her immense light is awakened to rise and vitalize all the chakras above. The second chakra, luminous orange, holds emotional and sexual intimacy needs as well as creativity and is located in the pubic bowl and belly. This area is also the base of what the Japanese call *hara*, our center of gravity and awareness strengthened by sitting in meditation. The third chakra, yellow, is above the navel around the solar plexus and is worldly personal power, will and ego. It is usual to spend one's life majoring solely in the swirling forces of the first three chakras.

Aspirants who dare to explore the four higher chakras after studying and nurturing the first three are admonished by many male yoga and Buddhist teachers that we may be destroyed by raising the fearsome powers of primal energy in Mother Kundalini. To maintain health and sanity, texts warn us to "master" the elaborate, harrowing and secret techniques of a guru with certified lineage. While my Ladies and I have indeed been shaken with *shakti*, we have never been lost — for long. We know the pursuit of divine Love incarnate is a life-long commitment and quest, one which irrevocably changes values and lives. Exploring sexual power with your eyes open and head clear can be ravishingly beautiful and intense; it can also liberate deep pain. She who gives light must endure burning. We have found one way to renew and center our energy is to double the sincerity and love, but especially to loosen our seriousness. It is said that the angels can fly because they take themselves so lightly. We let ourselves find the wellsprings of joy in opening our rainbow-petaled chakras, let their energy sing again and again to us, "Merry meet, merry part and merry meet again." Use your partner, visual symbols or oral chants and cries to "part" intense focus so it does not become hypnosis. And smile; it is not too good to be true.

Thus protected, let us move intrepidly and gaily up to the fourth chakra, the great heart chakra, bathed in the warm green aura of the life force Herself. (A favorite gardening book says: Substitute one iron molecule of blood with one of magnesium and it becomes chlorophyll.) In the green heart chakra is located deep peace,

67

compassion, renewal, and Universal love beyond all separation. The voice and throat chakra is the fifth, and it shines with azure, bright sky blue. It is the source of our ability to communicate, "vibrate," the visions of our higher self in the sound of integration. The sixth chakra, known as the "third eye" or the "eye of the guru," is deep *l'heure bleue* indigo and is focus, clairvoyance and mystic awareness. The seventh, the "crown chakra" at the top of the head, holds the brilliant, opalescent white spectra of all Light and opens to the powerful stream connecting us to the celestial source of Grace. Its opening may be represented as a thousand-petal lotus. At the center of its radiance is a tiny blue pearl, sparkling and scintillating. Within this pearl the size of a sesame seed are the million upon million universes of the entire cosmos.

My lover and I often begin the Rosary of the Chakras by cupping and rubbing the bases of each other's spines, grounding our roots and connecting them with Mother Earth to hold us on our journey's course. Then we lovingly explore the entire tree of the body as Kundalini bio-energy awakens to flow in a pillar of light from our spinal trunk into the myriad branches of our nerves and veins. In good time, we focus contemplative and physical meditation into our second chakras. Kissing, caressing and penetrating, slow and swift, deep and tantalizing, we raise the second chakra to the pulsing *"aura clitoridis,"* chronicled in women's ancient rites. By touch, we can direct the streaming circuit of sexual energy slowly up and around all the chakras, opening, opening the wheels of ecstasy. Slow, meditative touch helps to dissolve any blocked, crystallized energy, spreading, healing and vitalizing our powers. Each chakra's attributes transform and "step up" our moving erotic and spiritual energies.

We sometimes let these build by "watching" our breath, synchronizing it, or focusing on body fragrances. We "open-sense" to micro-sensations of touch, visual and aural detail. We may pause to pulse with the candlelight or to listen to the windsong. We often listen to a wonderful tape by Kay Gardner, "A Rainbow Path," which was composed to flow through and clear the chakras. Sometimes we ripple orgasms to "center" psychic soars and descents as we spiral the chakra garden. The more gently aware, open and relaxed we are, calming the mind of past and future phantoms, the more delightful, deep and healing our connection is.

There are many other sensual/sacred practices we have created to explore the Goddess' garden of the senses. "Touching the Heart Strings" is one and "Dance of Two Phoenix" and "Mother May I . . . " are others. Some lend themselves to group rituals. Some seem so intimate or taboo, I feel I need to be in a trusted relationship, or with an initiate. Others, like the "Rosary of the Chakras," are perfect for first-time love-making, when all the world is birthing to new adventure. Any time, anywhere, I need only remember that the Great Queen, the Laughing Androgyne, is every woman who comes to play hide-and-seek with me, her Loving Queen.

Concha: Liquid Love

Although I am a triple fire sign, when I was swept into what I call "the river" of Lesbian sexuality, I felt a primal, elemental transmutation. Making love with a woman, I become as liquid as the ocean. The rings of fire that whirl at my core seem to melt into warm, deep ripples dilating each cell. Is this because my first woman lover was a sea-witch?

I met Kemble one June morning on a "restricted" state island preserve off the south coast of Georgia. This was one of the "Golden Isles," named for the glow of dawn and twilight on the rippling marsh grasses. I had decided to try this wild, solitary place as a writer's retreat from teaching in Savannah while my husband worked with a three-man science team permitted to be on the ecologically protected island. Kemble and I quite startled each other that morning at dawn when I turned a curve of the shore to find a handsome silver-haired sailor illegally mooring her tiny boat. "Don't tell the boys," she winked, pointing to her boat's name, "No Trace," "and I'll ferry you all round these sea meadows." Kemble turned out to be a guide who took tourists and fishers out along Georgia's necklace of islands. Tourists sometimes thought the lithe, strong Kemble was a man with her hair tucked under her Greek sailing cap. She always smiled at them, "Am I the first lady pirate in your life?" Kemble lived lightly, if illegally, on one or another of the tour boats or pleasure craft moored in the marinas of the residential islands — when she wasn't enjoying the state preserve here.

We visited together on "our" island many mornings. She usually brought a Thermos to share of fire-gold tea which she held in a glass to the ocean sunrise. Kemble enjoyed my name, Concha, and would chant it with the names of all the other shells she found on the beach. When we said hello or good-bye, she would often put her lips near my ear and say, "La Concha, Concha, holds the inland sea . . . " Then, with a whoop, "May the flow be with you." She charmed and fascinated me. She knew Georgia's barrier islands and their vast

69

coastal marshes like a lover. She showed me the sea and plant life with the eye of a high-powered camera, with the magic of a fairy tale. Every rock harbored a mystery like a white ghost crab, every inlet a nymph. She recounted how the earth's now embattled tidal marshes are the great mothers of life, the fabulous ecosystem which births and nurtures the organic isotopes, microorganisms, algae and complex sea creatures that sustain the planet's entire aquatic food web. I remember her reverently squeezing the sticky black marsh soil teeming with microscopic life, breathing it in. "This is it, the dark Mother, the gooeyest of goo, the primordial cauldron."

I asked Kemble to come with us to one of the big resort islands to celebrate the Fourth of July weekend. One of the scientists from South Carolina, the fireworks factory of the nation, had invited everyone to see "the sky rain fire with some home-grown" at an oceanfront estate he'd rented for the long weekend on the nearby island. "Let's stay right here to celebrate Liberty," Kemble countered. "It's my fiftieth birthday. The great tide of Yin is coming and with her a billion fireflies." She laughed and whispered, "La Concha." This time she touched the little flaps of my ears and closed them gently. "Concha, Concha, listen to the ocean inside, the song of the fireflies, their tiny golden bells, the percussion of your heart." She held me this way several minutes; then, as I stammered to answer, she put her finger to my lips, smiled, and headed for her little boat.

Of course I stayed. I waited all July Fourth for her, wandering the island, feeling more and more like a fool. As it got dark, I walked out on the pier. Looking back toward shore, I saw, yes, millions of fireflies. They lit the old, twisted plantation oaks like faerie trees. Suddenly it began to pour, dousing their little lanterns and drenching me to the bone as I ran through torrents of warm rain. When I reached the house, Kemble was there, serenely sitting in the swing on our porch, a jar of fireflies beside her. "Come in," she said, "and let me lick the rain off you," like this was the most natural proposal in the world.

It was. She slowly undressed me, wine-tasting my whole body with her lips. I could hear our blood pulsing, beat for beat. Kemble set the fireflies free and scattered cinnamon bark and cedar on a little piece of burning charcoal, spicing and sparking the warm, open-windowed room. She massaged me with a few drops of citrus oil, first my crown, then my forehead, my hands, heart, breasts, vulva, thighs, and feet. As I touched the beautiful swirling creatures tattooed on her inner thigh, she began telling me of the realms of the *nagas*, serpent beings who guard treasures in underwater palaces and protect the books of mystic knowledge. The rain beat on the rain.

70

My vulva flooded with juices. My body felt fluid, with the warm liquid energy of ripe glistening fruit, of floral tissue, of dream and poem. Even my mouth began to water as Kemble kissed the delicate flesh of my inner lip and ran her tongue under the shaft of my tongue to drink at the well there. Our nipples and bellies and mounds kissed. Kemble whispered that with "deep beyond deep" kissing she would find my "T-spot," the place where the pool of nectar behind the forehead can be released onto the root of the tongue. This inner nectar washes and purifies the taste buds, so that ordinary food tastes like ambrosia. This nectar travels to the belly, then to the solar plexus, where it spreads through the nerves, making the whole body flow like warm amber.

As we kissed, we began to inhale one another's breath. "Keep your eyes open," she said, "go slow, go deep and flow wide." As we began to harmonize our breathstreams, I felt we were in almost telepathic communion, experiencing the other's waves of emotion and sensation. I began to feel, if not actually hear, her sing, "Concha, Concha, take a deep breath and *plunge*." I did. Entering, entering, entering . . . through tide pools of tide pools, into crimson, then darkening grottos. These slowly parted into bright, huge waves and widening horizons which melted into one as we came into a string of suns.

We sunned, explored, sipped, quaffed, and sucked each other like this for two more days. I was drunk on Kemble the whole summer, her tides, her stories, her body. "We water signs major in emotions," she said, "and if there's a mood to be set, we'll try." She made love poetically, feathering me to oblivion, tonguing one golden brown sugar crystal from the eye of a strawberry into my mouth. She could also be as practical as a calculator: "Let's breathe in 7:1:7 until we are easy," or, "Do you know the nine types of ladyfinger penetration, and the eight vaginal depths?" Since Savannah was only a couple of hours' drive from my Golden Isles tantrika, I made exuberant plans to see Kemble as often as possible once my teaching began.

I had forgotten one thing: Kemble was a sailor. She left the Golden Isles for the Keys, then the Texas Gulf, then San Francisco (why I came here), then Alaska (still loving me), now New Zealand . . . . We are water and flame: both persist, yet do not, depending on the conditions arising. Kemble used to quote *Even Cowgirls Get the Blues*: Since humans are 86 percent water, water obviously invented us to move itself around from one place to another.

She did leave the tide of Yin in me, a strong river reaching toward the great sea. "Never Turn Your Back on the Ocean," I can hear

Kemble reading triumphantly on all the official beach signs. So I opened my heart again. I took my next woman lover to honeymoon along every waterfall in the Columbia Gorge. Whenever I'm sweet on someone, I ask her, as soon as is prudent, to come swimming with me or to the sauna or hot tubs. Even if we never become lovers, or if she's straight, I can feel satisfied appreciating the incredible membrane of our flesh as a pliant bridge rather than a boundary, connecting the world touching us.

Anywhere I move, I furnish my bathroom as a "palace of Yin," with art, flowers, herbs, sachets, candles, feathers, bath crystals, body paints, oils, lotions and perfumes. The bigger the tub, the better (the bigger the bathroom, the better). Moveable shower heads are great for tickling your fancy with jetstreams. Little love spankings have their best wake-up sting on warm, wet flesh. I love to stand under the shower in conjugal embrace with a woman, the world moist and shining. Our temples rinsed and purified, we dry each other, then stand together visualizing crystal light pouring through our joined hands. My lover and I also bathe each other in water floating with rose petals, lavender, or with the scented geranium and verbena leaves I grow. We love bathing at night with candles and fire sticks of incense lit, a water and fire marriage. Fourth of July sparklers make fine "showers" in the tub too. (Be sure to open the window.) Since it would take ten to fifteen cases to take a bath in champagne, I haven't tried that yet; a one-bottle shower is fine.

But bring on the bubbles galore! Did you ever "bubble dance" a woman's nude body by blowing liquid pearls all over her? You can get little jars of bubble solution with a wand at toy and party stores. (In fact, lots of decorations and toys at party stores are especially festive in a small bathroom at night.) A secret of bubble blowing is never to hurry; blow *very* slowly through the little wand or pipe. I met a woman who could put a soap bubble around a flower. She placed a magnolia in the center of a lilac dinner plate and filled the plate with about an eighth of an inch of soapy water. She made a cone from the stiff paper of a grocery sack and placed it in the water over the magnolia. She then gently blew into the cone while slowly raising it from the plate. A bubble began to form under the cone as she blew and lifted it. Then she withdrew the cone very carefully, and — *voilà*, magnolia in a sphere of rainbows! She also showed me how to cut a bubble in two with a soapy knife. Naturally, I married this woman. We blow many a bubble metaphor about our relationship and the fleeting world, "a star at dawn, a bubble in a stream, a child's laugh, a phantasm of a dream," but our sense of wonder keeps flowing on — even through some ice blocks and exploding steam.

One of the most steamy, wondrous and exotic things to do with a lover is to slowly, carefully wash her feet in a bowl of warm, sudsy water or scented warm water and glycerine. Glycerine water is slippery and sexy, and you don't have to rinse it off. To bathe a woman's feet and anoint them with oil is a tender, cherishing act, one to totally melt the heart. The feet, like the hands, are covered with a multitude of highly sensitive nerve endings — 72,000 according to reflexology, the theory that stimulation of certain areas of the foot has an effect on corresponding organs and glands. But the feet, usually encased in shoes, or even hobbled in uncomfortable ones, rarely get sensory stimulation, not to mention gratification. It is the feet which make our connection with the earth, they are our very foundation. Surely everyone needs a little foot-loose loving?

In the amazing religion of "Boko-maru," described in the novel *Cat's Cradle* by Kurt Vonnegut, the touching of feet in a special foot ritual is the Bokononist act of eroticism, their mingling of awarenesses. "Bokononists believe it is impossible to be sole to sole with another person without loving the person, provided the feet of both people are clean and nicely tended." I have heard New York women say they could not possibly live in the city were it not for a regular foot massage and pedicure, and a certain glow comes into their eyes. Never underestimate the possibilities of a woman with gold sandals or manicured toenails — or one who invites you to "take off your shoes . . . "

The laying on of hands during massage not only relaxes tension and stimulates nerve points that may be congested, but between lovers becomes a transmission of intimacy and energy to one another. Massage is making love in slow motion. Even foot massage, seemingly so humble, is too powerful for many people to deal with. It is a dramatic way of showing — and accepting — empathy, care and great respect for one's total physical being. The massage technique you use is less important than the love, focus and imagination you bring, but here are a few footnotes I got from practitioners of reflexology.

First, how you feel about doing a foot massage is as important as how your lover feels about receiving it. Talk about the "act" and reaffirm your "Boko-maru" connection. Prepare by rubbing your hands together to feel the energy between them. Reflexologists usually recommend your partner be reclining so her spine is straight and that a pillow be placed under her knees so her legs are not locked. Make sure the rest of her body is good and warm. Try to talk only as necessary for feedback, in order not to interrupt the "sole connection" and cellular communications.

73

Keep your hands in continuous contact with her feet, so that even when you reach for more oil, one hand is on the foot maintaining connection. Besides full-hand stroking and kneading, thumb pressure in small circles feels good on the fleshy ball of the foot. The solar plexus reflex is just below the inner ball of the foot in a little crevice where the thumb fits perfectly. If reflexology is correct, stimulation here can open up the whole breathstream via the diaphragm as well as the many nerve passages. Gently pull and squeeze the toes, which in reflexology correspond to the head area and major nerves. Breathe, relax and pause when you hit a tender spot (you will) or if your lover is overcome by stimulus (not unusual); murmur, "How about letting go?" as you work more gently. Give her a whiff of something calm like balsam or oil of thyme you've soaked on a piece of cotton. If your hand feels heavy or tired, shake it out; try to let most energy flow *through* you rather than to or from you.

Be sure to kiss her toes as you finish, sucking them — if she can bear the ecstasy. The flesh between the toes is exquisitely soft and sensitive. Explore the classic Boko-maru position: sole to sole, legal even in Georgia. Now, you can start all over again, perhaps with the hands this time, bathing, oiling and massaging. Kemble said that in the lunar cycle a woman feels throughout her life, each of us has a unique part of the body to be honored and awakened each moon phase. At the full moon, I like "the kiss of enlightenment" all over my eyelids and forehead. Before my menses, I always love my earlobes rubbed and kissed. Earlobe rubbing is most relaxing and sleep-making after tongue and finger play there.

Women's sexuality is so outflowing and multi-vibrational that one of the most tantalizing of experiences is to "wonder" if we did, in fact, "make" love at all? This first happened to me standing hand in hand with Kemble in the ocean, our cunts moss-wet in the buffeting waves. A vortex in me quivered and deepened . . . I knew I came into the world not alone, but rather came out of it like a wave. Kemble drew me to her as though I had spoken aloud. We shared orgasms as the bubbles of jeweled spindrift opened to the sun . . . didn't we?

IV.
The Jealousy
Heartburn

NEVER ASK YOUR LOVER
HOW MANY WOMEN SHE'S SLEPT WITH...

The ironic price we seem to make ourselves pay for sexual pleasure is the fear of losing it. Jealousy is the most bitter of emotions because it is associated with the sweetest. Until we reach Buddhaland, it seems impossible to replace sexual jealousy with sexual generosity. Jealousy appears born in the human species, the most psychologically insecure and therefore controlling of all animals. If not inborn, jealousy is certainly fed by our relentless economic system. Certain Polynesian and pre-patriarchal societies, for example, appear to be fairly free of sexual jealousy, whereas corporate capitalism literally legalizes greed. We are encouraged to privately possess, not only all material objects, but even human beings, especially women. We are taught to live in a realm of scarcity, where continuous competition is essential to ever get what we need. This is so endemic that easily available or used goods, including women, are "cheapened."

Since our social model is dominance/submission, rather than partnership, its active agent is control, and its key attribute is jealousy. Works such as *When Society Becomes an Addict* by Anne Wilson Schaef reveal how social forces encourage us to become as addicted to a person or process as to a substance. But take heart. As cooperative Lesbian culture moves away from the patriarchy/capitalism/ addiction model, many Lesbians are understanding that jealousy is yet another residue of that old life. This means not that we can merely polish jealousy away, but that we don't necessarily have to let it corrode our relationships.

Believe it or not, some kinds of jealousy are useful. They can actually define and strengthen a relationship — if we change their panic and control context. Other jealousy, that of paranoid, totally imagined terrors, is a wild stew of love, hate, panic, and despair, where doubts are crueller than the worst truths. "Retro-jealousy," or *angst* over a lover's previous relationships, is another example of an ego off its rails. Physically violent jealousy, largely a male phenomenon, is also outside the scope of this household manual. (With violence, there is only one course available: press charges and move out.) Let us look at ordinary garden variety jealousy, the common cold of Lesbian relationships. As a social disease, it may be as useful as a cold can be useful — a time to slow down and re-value health.

Jealous feelings can arise in at least three different settings, which are sometimes combined for special challenge. In scenario number one, you are simply not meeting some of your lover's essential needs. You have asked or she has said so, and she thinks she has found someone who seems to be caring for her better. To get her back, you'll probably have to actually change a behavior or two. This is by no means easy, but the point is that things are so unsatisfactory between you and your lover that another woman has been enlisted for aid. "That woman" is your early warning system. She can rarely destroy a solid relationship, but she is used as the catalyst for change. She herself usually ignores her "pawn" role, having her own needs and hopes. Your first step is to find out exactly what is wrong! Example: You are too busy or preoccupied to be romantic; the other woman is aglow with attention. You allow yourself to be grumpy, critical and picky; the other woman rewards all your lover's good qualities and ignores the rest as not being worth her time and bother. This is the place for a soul-searching of your response-abilities, which a live relationship seems to demand.

In scenario number two, your lover's affair has very little, if anything, to do with your actions at all. She needs to find something in herself that is missing: self-esteem, excitement, success, applause, power, self-knowledge. Here you can only give her a big meadow, and above all — take care of yourself. "If you love something very much, let it go free. If it doesn't return, it wasn't meant to be yours. If it does, love it forever." Most women never intend a trial-balloon affair to decimate their primary relationship. Remember, the odds are in your favor if you play it right and don't panic. Above all, keep the priority: nurture and love yourself first in every way you can. Friends, treats, holidays. Be yin with her; go full yang for yourself.

In scenario three of "useful" jealousy, your own needs for security are not being met because the relationship's assumptions are unclear or are changing. You suffer a terrifying vagueness of whether your lover is coming or going. Perhaps you have never dared to discuss the spectre of "the other woman," so she is even more frightening. Maybe your lover has just finished years of school or a large project and has time for more people, or, because of new activities, is meeting many women in her life. So it becomes time for you to "define the territory," which is a form of tribute to a very special person and usually is a relief to everyone concerned. If your lover wants to talk triangles, set up each person's limits and protocol. Ask your lover if both of you can verbally or in writing draw up some kind of "accords" or a "covenant of commitment." In a relationship where "anything goes," nothing goes very well.

A covenant can mean simply settling as far as possible what each hopes the length or the type of the relationship will be. In your discussion or written accords, be sure to acknowledge what you love about each other — besides exclusive sex. Remember that erotic energy can deepen and inform all experience, whether it is exclusive or not. Focus on the gift and quality of the time you have together and what you want to do with it, not the time or sex being "taken away." Celebrate this positive "time sharing" and intimacy often. So what if your lover "sleeps out" 20 percent of the time (likely it is less than 2 percent)? How really deprived are you? She has not, after all, been doled out a finite number of kisses and caresses, swiftly to be depleted. Accept that there may be fly-by-nights, other sexual entertainers, even long-distance, long-term mistresses, but do not allow the mutual loss of much that is beloved to occur because you decide to play full-time proprietor. This makes you suspicious, rude and unattractive — the very qualities that will repel the woman you are afraid to lose.

Omnigamy

This leads us into one of the great debates within The*a*logica Lesbiana: whether to practice our faith in peaceful nunnery for two or to try to keep it alive in a tumultuous multistery of the "other women." The monogamy/nonmonogamy debate has probably raged since the Golden Age of the Great Goddess and will go on until the Last Great Wave, so we cannot hope to solve it here. Women, unlike men, do not tend to take sex impersonally or casually, so that's that. Let us simply present both views as represented in Lady Clitoressa's Circle.

Each of the women, a monogamist and a pluralist, has a different season of fashion. A few years back, our consultant on high fidelity, Constance, stood outside the trend, teased as the "cervical cop," the "sexual fundamentalist," a "sexual macrobiotic." But our matrimonialist held to her commitment and prospered. Constance and her lover have an agreement, a "woman's honor code," to be sexually intimate with only one another, maybe not forever, but until one of them directly states that she wishes to "open the circle" — not break it. Each is to give the other one notice *before* the act, and then the matter will be up for discussion. (Such discussion has already clarified and strengthened the relationship.) Promiscuity will not necessarily be a terminal issue; with time the relationship may be stable enough to handle it.

Deep peace and security reign. These loyalists are "freed up," at least of diversionary outsiders, to build a strong relationship now, the only time we ever have to enjoy. There is independent time to focus on individual friendships, professions, pastimes, instead of roller coaster intrigues. Constance quotes Miss Manners: "Monogamy was created to give people a rest. We must celebrate a species of grown-up who is sufficiently evolved to derive pleasure from knowing she can rely on another's love instead of seeking the cheap excitement of uncertainty." Constance and her lover smile into each other's eyes: "Trust is the most powerful aphrodisiac."

But let us hear from the libertine Scarlett, a rover whose only sexual vow is, "My heart is reserved for questers. I cannot be faithful to others, only to myself." Scarlett feels stifled rather than secure in a closed circuit. She flourishes with a palette of sexual relationships to express herself and learn about life. Scarlett, like most pluralists, is a fatalist, recognizing how very transient monogamous relationships are, that most Lesbians love in "serial monogamy," not forevers. A survey in *Lesbian Passion* shows our average relationship stay is around three years. As San Francisco comedian Marga Gomez jokes, "My lover and I joined a support group for 'Lesbians in Monogamous Relationships.' It was great — until she met someone there." Scarlett believes it doesn't matter whether you champion monogamy or pluralism because you will do whatever you want to do anyway. If you don't, your lover will.

Scarlett does not equate multiple sexual adventures with moral turpitude, but with sexual positivism and discovery. She is as honest and committed a lover/friend as any monogamist. With only a short-term lease among the stars, why be afraid to browse? "Is there only one star, *my* star, on whom I can and must depend for light?"

The issue, says Scarlett, is more one of responsibility, honesty, and, above all, timing. "Watch the quick impulse." The problem with promiscuity is *careless* love, lack of a policy openly stated and as sensitive to everyone's needs as it can be. This calls for some guidelines concerning safe sex, territory and time allotment, "important days," and veto power. Having one's feet in a couple of boats takes consummate balance, or there is tumultuous upset, painful and unfair to everyone. A rake's life takes oceans of discussion, boiling down to a Witch's brew of honesty and discretion combined.

The pluralist must also be one of the most reassuring and eloquent women on earth to assuage a lover's pain over unfaithfulness. Any defensiveness and anger show her up for a mean spoiler, not a great lover. If you insist on playing the "love the one you're with" game: focus. Convince the hurt woman you love just how much you do love her. Invest effort to more than equal what you just spent in dalliance. Your heart is otherwise too poor to afford cheap thrills.

The confirmed pluralist usually does not have a live-in relationship with her primary lover because of the jealousy and pain even peccadilloes can cause. Totally open marriages seem to require separate living spaces, or acres of privacy. Note one reason the liberated women in the feminist utopias like *Wanderground* by Sally Gearhart and *Woman on the Edge of Time* by Marge Piercy can enjoy multiple relationships is because they live privately. This is why Lady Clitoressa says that "non-monogamy is less a moral problem than a housing issue." She adds that non-monogamy usually occurs in direct proportion to how much discretionary time one can afford. It makes sense, for example, that a woman working a demanding full-time job with an artist's career on the side and three young children may opt for monogamy. Scarlett emphasizes that, ironically, the most successful wantons probably spend most nights in bed alone because they don't live with a primary lover. "Players bow out fast if you don't take vows." But she prefers it that way. "Why should I limit the variety of my sexual practice because of fear of being alone? Things done only because of anxiety create more anxiety. I won't let fear limit my experience and puritanize my natural patterns of love."

Constance and Scarlett are admittedly "best" scenarios, Lesbians liberated by their inclinations. But we all know bonded monogamists; neutered as tree stumps, fearful, insulated couples trying to close the door on existential realities such as loneliness and change. We also know pluralists who can only kiss and run, addicted to fantasy and the ego boost of "conquest," women too weak and dishonest for any kind of responsibility and commitment. Every lifestyle, every faith, however, has its losers and abusers and cannot be judged solely on these. Why someone is pluralist or monogamist at certain phases of her life and which role is "correct" are not the issues. The real question is what is the *effect* of either behavior on an intimate relationship? Do the players grow together or limit their potential by the practice? Oddly, pluralists and monogamists seem to attract one another, or in a couple's changing tides, one plays one role, then the other, rarely at the same time (groan). The willingness in a relationship to accept both philosophies as holding value can lead to the rare, sensitive state Lady Clitoressa calls "omnigamy."

Honorable Pluralism

Let's say you wish to consider appearing in the Great Theater of Omnigamy, the mythological Extended Couple starring in Open Marriage, or, even, that you stumble into a brief encounter once every three years. How can pluralism create more love than trouble in the world? Pluralism often does cause more trouble than it is worth because the roving eye forgets two matters of the heart: honor and compassion. Lady Clitoressa's question is a searching one: "Cannot pleasure be kind?" Kindness, unfortunately, can be as inconvenient as good manners, demanding concentration and consideration for another's needs by being patient with your own. Honest and satisfying pleasure probably does make us kind. But if you are having an affair as revenge against your lover, to manipulate someone, because your life feels bleak or powerless, because you want to be punished, or for any one of the futile, sadder reasons people have sex, more is lost than gained.

If there are already such ongoing problems, there will usually be lies to cover up the mess you are making by adding the complication of sex. We lie to escape consequences. Consequences may indeed be harsh if you have not put in or are not willing to make the effort and time to reassure your old lover and sympathize with her pain. Sex *per se* is an honest, honorable form of communication and a fine vehicle of mutual self-interest. As such it is precious and powerful, but it is never "free." Lady Clitoressa avers that "free love" — no consequences, no responsibility, no code — is a fraud on the scale of "Atoms for Peace." We also lie because we are afraid our lover will know who we really are. Then, as liars, we are even more ashamed and contemptuous of ourselves. Outright lies, falsification and distortion make everyone feel lousy. Everyone. It takes a long time to build trust, but ten times as long to rebuild it once betrayed.

The Ladies of Lady Clitoressa's Circle, honorable women all, often discuss the subtlety and paradox of a workable code of pluralism. How to conduct ourselves as "blessed infidels," and maintain what the Buddhists call the "right speech" of truth? The Ladies say total honesty is as rarefied a concept as total non-violence and may not always be possible or even wise. Compassion, after all, is as much a part of one's integrity as honesty. Compassion asks you to consider who else pays the price for your total, raw honesty. With most people, the limits of honesty are probably reached most quickly over infidelity than any other issue. Studies of heterosexual couples working toward completely honest relationships show that only 10 percent are able to deal with unconditional honesty regarding infidelity. Lesbians may be tougher, but how many?

82

The Ladies say, "Too much reality can sometimes be too much of a good thing." Skilled communication or "clean process" does not mean you always tell everyone everything about everyone and everything. Save your breath. Face the fact that sexual encounters are often sheer, trifling frivolity. Frivolity has its own value, but swollen with meaning it is not. Perhaps the greatest honesty is admitting to your own soul that both you and your lover are riddled with all kinds of folly. Frivolity can be the froth of life. Drink or blow it from the cup, but why belabor it?

Many women actually prefer to look away from a partner's infidelity, to notice but not to watch. They know something is going on, but do not intend to wearily play prosecutor — or to sanction the affair either. As the *I Ching* says, "The Superior Woman lets many things pass without being duped." These are usually pretty secure women with lots of self-esteem, who take a "this too shall pass" attitude and pack a "Jealousy First Aid Kit." Meanwhile, of course, they are getting what they minimally need or much, much better. Some put themselves on the record once and for all that their partner's promiscuity hurts them, that it can spoil good things, and that they need extra consideration when this happens. The profligate who is without the finesse to make her affair as inconspicuous as possible in this case is simply cruel and abusive. You never need be caught in *flagrante delicto*, or even slightly rumpled, unless you are actually seeking attention or containment — or are a true bumpkin. Do not ever assume, however, that your lover does not know or suspect that you are stepping out. Women are, after all, the radar queens. Your lover is probably invoking her privilege of tact. Afford her the same, or you do not have the skill to play a game of nerves.

One code to live up to in this delicate area is to answer as honestly and *gently* as you can when directly questioned about infidelity. You have the right of privacy, even the obligation to be silent about details, but admit the affair. Your lover has asked for reality. Any lie will lead to ongoing craziness for you both. Here is the critical time to be especially honest and energetic with your primary lover about your feelings of love for her and to try to arrange something tolerable for both of you. She deserves that. Be prepared to let this new lover go. There is always another, you rogue.

If never questioned about the affair, why in the world subject anyone to compulsive disclosure, especially over nascent, unconsummated flings or finished ones? Again, who really pays the price for your "honesty"? If it is "right speech," your words are motivated by compassion. Alternatively, if you insist on acting the part of an intrusive, possessive and controlling lover, you may be setting

83

yourself up for — or deserve — the torments of the damned. For example, fueled with jealousy, it is pure self-abuse to read another's journal or letters to discover something. There goes all peace of mind *and* self-esteem. Which brings us to Lady Clitoressa's:

Five Questions Never to Ask Your Lover

1. When I was gone, did you make it with someone else?
2. Have you ever wanted to make love with . . . ?
3. Do you get hot for anyone except me?
4. How many women have you slept with?
5. Have you ever lied to me?

The "Five Questions Never" is also called "maintaining a noble silence." Noble silence provides a serenity beyond words.

A Jealousy First Aid Kit

Even wise and tactful omnigamists pack a "Jealousy First Aid Kit" for safety when the pleasure centers stop firing moonbeams and the dark emotions demand their turn. Note well: an emergency first aid kit will never "cure" jealousy, but it can minimize infection and even prevent relationship death.

First and foremost, do not be paranoid. Always assume your lover is faithful until she proves she is not. No circumstantial evidence, please. Trust can beget honesty since prophecies often fulfill themselves. Show your appreciation for her fidelity by often reminding your lover how honored you are to be the one to share her bower when you know a whole world of women is dying just to open the door.

When your lover has obviously strayed, then deal with jealousy as you would any difficult emotion: truly admit it is there and it hurts. Freeze it or feign indifference and generosity, and you will get an emotional meltdown later which cannot be contained. Don't blame or even judge yourself for being anxious, hurt or angry. Consider jealousy a wound, like a blade passing through the heart. You could only have prevented it with no heart at all. You are hit. That is the way it is. Social people get social diseases.

Next, focus unwaveringly on the jealousy itself, again without judgment. This takes strong energy, summoning vital forces, so breathe in power. Watch the jealousy. Feel its qualities: chilling, fiery, crushing, all of these? Finally, label it: "Jealous." "Jealous." Inhale your power and exhale acceptance. Oddly enough, in the very act of labeling an emotion, you can feel your awareness momentarily unhook and detach from it. Jealousy is flooding through you, but YOU are not jealousy. You HAVE jealousy. The distinction is both profound and freeing. Your serene "core of stillness," as named by Lesbian poet Elsa Gidlow, watches emotions like jealousy flow by like the storylines of a film, but is not hypnotized by them. Elsa found her core of stillness alone, which in deep poverty and love loss prevented her from committing suicide. She said this "invisible axis, no-motion at the center of motion — and emotion" is where invulnerable healing powers lie. If you breathe ever more deeply and take your core of stillness to the Eternal Core, well, my dears, you will be on the gospel train ready to make friends with life again.

Maybe your quest isn't so bad. Here you are, courting the cosmos with your best lover, yourself, the vital being you never have to worry about losing. Notice that no one can ever "take your place," even "compete" with your unique, precious self. You are one of a kind, a wondrous blend of qualities and gifts. Your significance is an absolute, a legitimacy beyond the validation of another. You are irreplaceable or you would not have been called to the blue planet. Here you most definitely are. Take careful stock of the singular gifts and the life experiences you brought to share and develop. Perhaps jealousy is the quest for our own self-assurance and self-appreciation. We each have purposes far beyond any lover's whims of the moment. We each have munificent powers to share beyond self and one other. It is a big sky. Enjoy your garden of undiminished special purposes and powers. Your lover cannot forget them if you do not.

So here you are awakened and rested, fed and watered. Be patient with yourself; you only slowly re-energize your powers after exhausting them over someone else's dalliance. By this time your lover's affair may have blown over, a folly you were too busy in "core" contemplation to ever embarrass yourself in. Let the dead bury the dead. Forgive and thankfully forget it. But suppose we have an ongoing soap opera? *Basta ya!* Enough! The time has come for the breathless resolution before closure. Enter [clashing of cymbals]: Warrior Woman. You are ready to unfurl your heart and confront each character in this little drama with your "Here I Stand."

Always make it a practice to inform the other woman directly how you feel just as soon as you feel coherent and self-possessed. She can't read your mind and may have been slipped a lot of non-sense by your obviously errant lover. You have nothing to lose by briefly confronting her, and everything to gain. Clarity works wonders to dispel *angst*, remove unwarranted doubts, and set the record straight. You put everyone on notice that you are no pushover, that you are a force to be reckoned with, that your rights and feelings count.

Simply call the woman to ask her what in the world her intentions are with your "partner." Say that you do not understand what is going on and repeat that you want to know her intentions. Stop and listen carefully here. Do not be hasty, nasty or blaming. This is a communication call. Remember also that your lover is damnably attractive. If you could fall for her, why not someone else? It is best not to react at all to the other woman's excuses except to calmly repeat, "I see," or variations thereof. You may get a lot of information or nothing at all. It does not matter. If you let yourself react to the other woman's stuff, you get stuck in her agenda, which is decidedly not yours. Your aim is to put her on the spot and for her to consciously take some responsibility for her actions. She is *not* responsible for your freak-out; that's your baby. Only one person is responsible for your jealousy and its management: you.

Move on to the most important point. Tell her you appreciate her honesty and that you must be honest with her. Give her the truth to live with: you are deeply in love with your partner and are terribly hurt and confused by their actions. You don't know yet what you are going to do, but you want to give her the respect of a hearing. End of conversation. No hysterics. No loss of face. No verbal violence or flying debris. In a potentially harmful situation, you are a clarifying rather than destructive force. This deserves respect.

Such a point-blank conversation will scare off most women or be the wedge to crack their little idyll with grim reality. A great gesture, if you have the money, is to mail the parvenu a one-way ticket out of town. You can also send her a mock-up of a ticket or an appropriate card. Nothing vicious, just a refreshing flex of muscle. You may as well defend your desires and get a little fun out of all this muddle. The derivation of the word "jealousy" from the Greek *zelos*, meaning zeal, suggests *action* regarding something precious. It is not forever feeling your feelings feel while everyone else is setting the context.

Of course, the other woman may be herself a jealous and determined "couple cracker" or a person who feeds on messy conflict for excitement. Such a one is a waste of breath and energy to relate to more than once, a tar-baby of a rival. Henceforth, ignore her, or you'll be stuck in a hell of meetings, recriminations, and torturous experiments of emotional cannibalism.

Now move on to your lover, the one you want to relate to. Inform her you have talked with the other woman; reveal only the fact that you were honest with one another. Tell your lover the heart-truth too: you love her and are afraid of losing her. You have the rich history of a real alliance on your side. Remind her of every wondrous event you have shared and weathered. Naturally you are holding her hand without a hint of possessiveness. Let there be no doubt that you love and want her. No neediness, no false pride either. Win her back with your love; do not destroy things in anger and blame. Some wayward women stray for just this moment of feeling so carefully valued. You feel better, and come out looking pretty attractive under fire. You exhibit the very qualities we doubt the other woman possesses. Always consider the long haul when you begin to become irrational and violent with words and actions. You are not a madwoman to escape from. Be the woman someone wants to come back to when she wakes up, whether as lover or intimate heart-friend with a continued destiny. In the most generous spirited action of all, "humor" the situation. To be able to laugh, especially to smile at your own antics, shows great courage.

Rest your case. Leave your lover alone, for a long time if necessary. You have done everything you can. Be patient. Life herself is your sweetheart. Remember *Lady Clitoressa's Third Law of Motion: Women come and go; mainly they come.* If you have done your best, maintained some dignity, made a discovery, returned some good faith for bad, you have won. Lady Clitoressa promises that you will thus be granted the fervent wish all of us have, "Call her by my name."

V.
Beyond
Breakfast:

The Lesbian Love Relationship

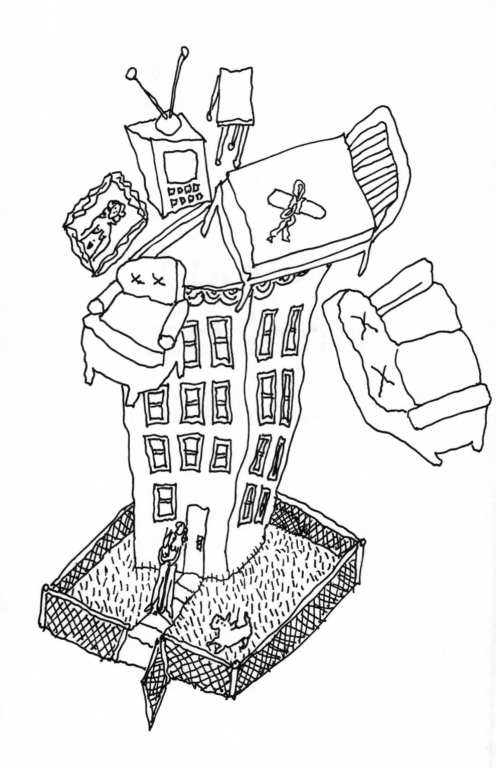

While erotic courtship may be the marvelous catalyst for a love relationship, it cannot be confused with The Great Union. One is bloom, one is ripeness; one romance, one realism. As in the flowering world, each cycle is beautiful in itself.

Patriarchy rarely focuses on the love union as a saga of work, power balancing and process. Rather, it spends colossal amounts of money and hype to goad us into the relentless addiction to the "chase." In contrast, Lesbians devote a great deal of time and energy to "Building the Relationship," trying not only to fall in love but to stay there. This is an exhilarating, infuriating, high investment since attraction and arousal do not necessarily lead to co-creation and commitment. But women are, after all, the undisputed relationship builders of humanity. Perhaps we are biologically wired to have stronger feelings of attachment than men in order to nurture children and to steward the planet. To draw on neurochemical studies again, we do know that stable relationships increase production of the body's calming happiness hormones, opiates like the endorphins. Perhaps such chemical production or its transmission/receptor sites are more developed in women, the reason two women together can alchemize phenomenal "contact highs," especially in co-habitation. Women ask, why allow erotic love energy to dissipate its vast power in mere lust, into joint egoism or into neglect when we can *build* something? And we try; Goddess, how we try.

This being the case, why are many Lesbian relationships rather short-lived? One massive survey on white, educated couplehood, *American Couples,* by professors Pepper Schwartz and Philip Blumstein, found Lesbian couples break up more frequently than married hets, live-in hets or even gay men. Naturally, a major reason for this is that unlike heterosexuals, many Lesbian lovers must live as society's outlaws, a not particularly stabilizing situation. Mainstream society, using its social, economic and political forces to vigorously uphold the overt and covert heterosexual contract, accords Lesbian couples no models or social sanction, much less any support. For overkill, it threatens Lesbians with loss of job, children, physical safety, status, and family of origin ties. You would think Lesbians are radioactive. The Duke of Windsor, giving up the throne of England "for the woman I love," is pale stuff compared to the heavy punishment and terrible pressure all kingdoms still inflict upon us giving up heterosexual privilege "for the woman I love." Does compulsory heterosexuality rule with such force because it is too unnatural to reign without it?

While such outside pressures can be devastating on a relationship, the Lesbian class, like all oppressed minorities, is hardest on itself. It takes inordinate independence and sophistication not to internalize at least a vein of self-hatred from our puritanical past and all the present social needling. Lesbians need to be detoxed from the notion that we do not "deserve" fulfilling relationships, and should settle for the dumps. Gay liberation and feminism have helped hugely to dispel such programming. With feminism, however, came a now common flip side to the program. Lesbians often go defiantly to its extreme opposite: we set our expectations heartbreakingly high. We fall into the fiction that an ideal, changeless state of being will automatically appear because women's natural passion, nurturance and empathy will perfectly merge in the light of mutual erotic preference. Here, little acceptance is accorded to, or preparation made for, our natural power struggles, jealousy, fusion/autonomy issues, sheer difference in life experience, tastes, social boundaries or personal habits. Also, because women have the sense to bond erotically, it does not necessarily follow that we instantly drop each of the less wise games we learned in het-land which seem to make life easier, but actually make it crazier, such as addictions, the scarcity mentality, intolerance. Additionally, feminist politics and philosophy now validate a quality already strong in Lesbians — love of independence. Many Lesbian feminists may well value independence over a relationship, if they must choose.

Another reason for Lesbian break-up is "the other woman." Lesbians do not yet weather extramarital affairs with aplomb, with either the pragmatism of heterosexual women nor the easy resilience of gay men. To most Lesbians sex is not terribly casual; it is an emotionally charged experience. Therefore, we often allow an outside affair to precipitate a major loyalty shift or to signal big changes. Lesbians have highly emotional reactions to dalliance, unlike men adept at "tricking," who are often unconscious of a lover's name or even face.

Some radical Lesbian therapists theorize that the Lesbian "roll-over" or "serial monogamy" may actually be healthy, or certainly deserving of no stigma. The real question may be not "Why do Lesbians break up?" but "How do so many Lesbians manage to stay together so passionately — so often?" If many of us deeply share our lives and passion with a different woman each decade, who is poorer?

Each great love is a new gift and teacher. And if we keep many of our lovers as heart-friends, what a clan. It is also true: "An army of ex-lovers cannot fail."

Lesbians are, despite the harassment of the empire, becoming pioneers in building mind-feeling, heart-thinking relationships. Like utopian communities who experimented with freeing and revising sexual mores, like all the feminist sexual pioneers before us (Sappho, Victoria Woodhull, Emma Goldman, Margaret Sanger, etc.), Lesbians are making love's journey freed of traditional boundaries, exploring new ways to relate in greater happiness and honesty. We have done an amazing job, especially since we must make up most of the guidelines as we go along and have had a safe opportunity to share and refine ideas for such a brief time in history. Relationship, not the simple lust model, nor the power-over model, not even the courtly "should be," but the deeply textured, multitoned, more radically beautiful love of acceptance and co-creation, is much discussed, if never quite defined, in Lady Clitoressa's Circle. Who can really define the joy as it flies? Here are a few ideals and definitions the Ladies traded about love relationships. All could agree on only one aspect: a love relationship is *created*, not found. Of the following statements from the Ladies concerning relationships, one is avowedly from a Hallmark greeting card to keep the list from being in any way authoritative.

The Body of a Relationship

A relationship is not a body at all, but a form of energy — moving, changing in cycles of renewal and recess.

A love relationship is not the same as "having." Love is not a needy "fix-me," nor even a "fair" deal. It does not possess, it liberates. Love is letting go.

A lover in a relationship is self-sufficient — "on my own, but not alone." She is more responsive than reactive to her beloved.

A relationship is interdependent, co-creative and *inter*penetrating, with liberty and justice for all — not just me.

A relationship is safe and receptive, respectful and courteous. It needs no defense, no pretense, just open disclosure. It is a big relief.

A love relationship has to find laughter every day because it is not happiness ever after.

A relationship says, "Love everyone because you love me."

A relationship is the tender hope of sustaining two oscillating forces — to merge and to be free — without ever trying to resolve them.

A relationship is social yoga, a mutual path of Awakening — to yourself.

A love relationship is physical excitement, physical comfort, physical companionship and physical work. It may mean tending the beloved, serving as her very eyes, legs and arms if need be.

A love relationship is not understanding and acceptance, but simply the ability to watch. It is the ability to watch which takes understanding and acceptance.

The Lesbian Relationship Spectrum

Lesbian relationship scholars★ can categorize our relationships on a scale of intimacy from one to infinity, beginning with the fairly accessible petting partner (no small blessing) through the favorite mistress (of many ceremonies) to emerge as full-blown Lover/Sister/Mother/Daughter/Holy Spirit. Any taxonomy breaks down because many couples display as many as ten relationship categories even before breakfast. Lady Clitoressa's final attempt to characterize the Lesbian mating cycle lists six major, often interconnecting, varieties of relations. "It is not particularly easy to become facile in any one of them," she notes with a shrug. "So come out early in life."

Courtship

Relationship as romantic, sensual enchantment — *le grand peut-être*, the great *perhaps* of shared vision. In a chemistry that defies science, each woman's feelings are created largely from within, having little to do with the true attributes of the "loved" one. Courtship is usually Act I of the Relationship Saga; hope is queen and drama is her court.

Liaison

Comes in hemi-, demi-, semi-, or full (monogamous). Sexual lovers are still under the Ninety-Day Warranty of Idealization, with their passion hopefully being enriched by some measure of compassion. They may be building a shared inner life, but a liaison still has the giddiness and uncertainties of spring. Time is spent

★ See the especially thoughtful therapists' books *Lesbian Couples* by D. Merilee Clunis and G. Dorsey Green and *Permanent Partners: Building Gay & Lesbian Relationships That Last* by Betty Berzon.

largely on the fields of romance, rather than on the rugged shores of reality. A "universe for two," when friends are shamefully neglected. If severed, leaves few roots, but perhaps a scar or two.

The Live-Apart Couple

Although "couple" interestingly enough is a singular word, the live-apart love couple is a bit more pluralistic than the live-in partnership. It has many of the qualities of "partnership," but decisions may not be as interdependent or destiny-oriented as with live-ins. Besides "the relationship," major energy may be directed to fulfilling one's worldly gifts, work or selfhood. There may be some relationship quandaries, but at least no hidden agendas by this stage. Each woman usually needs a great deal of separate time, while maintaining deep couple connection. Likely to value diversity and surprise or need acres of solitude, the women thrive in living apart. With two love nests, they do not need to modify as many trivial personal habits or preferences. They have distance from each other's friends or in-laws or old lovers. They may have brief, discreet flings with other women, happily returning to coupledom for sharing the most important parts of self.

Live-In Love Partners

Have "plighted their troth," or pledged their truth, major love energy, time, and interdependence to one another, perhaps in ritual ceremony. Since the women live together, they are usually monogamous to keep the peace. They seem to have a serenity of purpose or "destiny" and plan significant future hopes and goals together. The women are at least beyond denying, if not yet solving, differences of life experience and conflicts of power. In the highest realm, a magnificent, multi-gifted force based on trust and reliance. In lower realms partners tend to lose the "I" in "we." Partners often have enough mutuality to last beyond the average Lesbian relationship of three years, although a partnership cannot be defined by the time, only by the quality of caring. Partners often behave like ordinary, responsible adults and draw up wills and powers of attorney. They may behave like extraordinary, response-full adults and commit together to a spiritual path.

The "Après-Deux" Family

These are loving women who are no longer, or very minimally, sexually involved and have emerged from couplehood to become trusted "family" (a rare phenomenon in the het-set, even when children are involved). Such Lesbians are not mere "former" lovers because deep love abides between these heart-friends. They may still be romantic, flirtatious, even sensuous, but the key note here is "sisterly." A stout measure of acceptance and of gentle detachment toward one another leads to good humor; shared memories and history lead to great tenderness. An often initially difficult relationship, since old wounds must heal, *après-deux* is one of Lesbiana's most highly evolved and prized states of relationship. Could this be what couplehood actually aspires to, the *après-deux* cult of *"grandes amitiés"* (great friendships)? Again, let Natalie Barney set the standard: "I am very lazy when it comes to friendship. When I give it, I don't take it back." Natalie even constructed a great altar to friendship, her famous *Temple à l'Amitié*. This small, Greek-style temple in her garden was the visual focus of her weekly salons dedicated to friendship and creativity.

A distant cousin of *après-deux* is *alumnae*, the bittersweet bond two women share who have both been lovers with the same woman. Your relationship with the woman who is currently with your former lover? Color it a compassionate rose.

Compañeras/Passionate Friends

Compañeras are live-in or live-apart, deep-hearted, long-time friends. Intimate, emotional, affectionate involvement actualizes their joint ventures whether in great conversation and dining ("can be better than making love"), building a business, raising children, square dancing, supporting a cause, making a convivial home. Theirs is a marriage of companionship and sharing for optimum enjoyment, satisfaction and commonwealth. The passion is emotional rather than sexual, but may be up to its roses in romanticism, as in many "Boston marriages," or may be based on shared spiritual ardor as in a women's *sanga, satsang* or convent. You can joyfully live without a lover, but you cannot really survive without a *compañera* to love. As Lady Clitoressa avers, "It is not the unmarried who are alone, it is the unloving."

Let us pause here for the Single Lesbian — half of us are, after all, and many are exuberantly happy, complete and fulfilled, thank you. (Perhaps they're not reading this book?) Why the relentless, even desperate, obsession to couple up? How else could we be using all the creative energy we spend in "the chase" — or in couple counseling? Never kid yourself; you simply trade the hassles of being single with a whole new set of problems in being married. Perhaps in the relatively young history of Lesbiana, *à deux* is just a phase, an old het-lover? When will we get the Noah's Ark syndrome out of our system?

Read *A Passion for Friends: Toward a Philosophy of Female Affection* by Janice Raymond. Passionate friendship is a way to have the best of both worlds — without a single's loneliness or a couple's craziness. Why do many Lesbians continue to value friendships as quite secondary to lover relationships? As Lady Clitoressa once remarked, "Friendship renews, while sex can be the most tiring thing in the world." At least in friendship we are freed from the delusion of trying to make sex do the work of love and love do the work of sex.

Despite the basic human need to consider one's love life "resolved," truly successful practitioners of all the above relationship varieties may act like their present type of relationship is permanent, but they never really consider it to be so in their heart of hearts. They know any relationship is for "time-being." No guarantees. This is not benign cynicism, but an awareness that every living phenomenon grows and changes. Boundaries reform, bridges appear, and, inevitably, all passes into the light. Your great lover and heart-friend is already dead, so leave nothing loving undone or unsaid. Such an awareness is not all sad. It enriches our capacity to share and taste time-being in all its vibrancy, to recognize each small moment of love as a miracle in the midst of self-interest and despair.

Stages of the Relationship Cycle

"It's just a stage — whether in life or relationships," say Lesbian relationship mavens. As we enter the swirling Theater of Relationship, organizing its changing processes into somewhat predictable evolutionary states or "passages" can increase equanimity, if not totally eliminate the inchoate helplessness we feel as a relationship goes kittywumpus. Acknowledging passages can help you to take the long view and free you from assuming that what you see now — roses or thorns — is all there is, can be, or will be. This simple allowing, watching things unfold, removes a lot of pressure from "The Relationship."

A good relationship is, after all, a living, changing confluence of two lives creating destiny. It is like the meeting of two rivers, both shaping each other and the common relationship ground they touch. Infinite tides are possible, but here are the five general relationship stages Lady Clitoressa's Circle approximately agree upon as having lived through. Note: the following cycles do not proceed one after another in neat steps. You may sow the seeds of one stage never to see it go anywhere else. You may — consciousness being as elastic as it is — experience cycles almost simultaneously. You may, of course, buck back into a formerly experienced state if your stars so dictate, your buttons are pushed, or the moon is high. A cycle may continuously repeat itself, be it in troublesome or enlightened ways. Take heart: the veterans of two or three long-term marriages say each consecutive relationship becomes easier to harmonize. According to *Lady Clitoressa's First Law of Relationships: We learn to love by watching how unloving we are.* Corollary: Be on the lookout for a silver-templed Lesbian on the stroll who is a long-distance relationship runner. Some of us can even provide references . . .

Stage One: First Blush

This is the passionate stage of "could be." You have found a woman to whom you believe you may be able to open your heart. The immensity of this discovery creates such mood alterations, joy and awe that First Blush is the most renowned and mythologized of all relationship stages. Lady Clitoressa's Circle discusses it endlessly, but since we already dedicated the entire first chapter to fantasyland, suffice it to repeat that things in First Blush are definitely on the upswing, hot and heavy. There is also a lot of ambiguity and confusion, but we edge that aside. We also push away conflict. Similarities between lovers are so accentuated that compatibility is nourished at the expense of real differences. What a perfect blend we are. This rose-colored existence may last from two weeks to two years. Gather ye rosebuds while ye may. Plunge deeper and deeper into the garden because one day — O Dark Goddess — you will find yourself thrashing in a grim thicket, chock-full of thorns. Welcome to:

Stage Two: Power Struggle

If First Blush is "could be," Power Struggle is "should be." Stage Two can last a few weeks or fill two lifetimes with bickering. Along that garden path, something happens to the perfect blend. Inevitably, we leave the land of Romance and cross the border into Reality. In this rough frontier, each lover's individualism finally bursts out: stark raving naked. Each woman begins to notice her beautiful and shining lover is (gasp!) beset with imperfections and (ugh!) free will. What a betrayal of pet projections and self-interest! Faults range from annoying personality quirks to full-blown tragic flaws of heroic proportions. You can't even agree about what time to go to

98

bed anymore. As Lady Clitoressa says, "The opposite of love is not hate but egotism." Now that you have each bequeathed your precious "love," you decide in one of the great uninvited power ploys of human nature that you each have the divine right to become one another's most informed critic and change-agent. While you will stop at nothing to make her over, she is too busy redesigning you to submit to the personality lube-job of your intentions. Each deputy of defense forms her own vigilante society to protect herself and to enforce control of the relationship. The "lovers" now treat each other worse than they would strangers. Where our mission was once to affirm, it is now to judge.

Besides attempts to remodel each other's personalities, Power Struggle is the phase where conflict over "issues" begins to rear its head. As opinions finally clash, we begin to feel less in control, and for some reason, less valued. One woman may now want to reclaim her distance; the other wants even more closeness. There may be conflict in dealing with money, work and leisure, conflict over children or being "out." Different views regarding sexual frequency and fidelity, over class, race or politics finally emerge. Hell's a'poppin'. Friends are wringing their hands. The cats don't come home anymore. Couple counselors are making big bucks. The beckoning oasis of the "other woman" shimmers on the horizon. It is fork-in-the-road time. You can now obey your left-brain, discriminating mind and break off the relationship. This way you are free to relentlessly pursue your eternal quest for perfection. We thus jump from relationship to relationship like mood to mood, and Power Struggle is the stage where most relationships end.

Or you decide this time to follow the lantern in your heart. You remember that love is a process, a process of refining your truths and realities, a process that is not conditional on meeting all your gratifications. You may viscerally feel the old troubadour verse, "Mortal love is but the licking of honey from thorns," but you shrug off the pain with a generous smile. Somewhere in the background you hear the old Lezzie country and western song: "Another Grade B movie on life's big silver screen,/ But the Queen of Hearts, she always finds the creme." You decide to not yet forsake the field, and instead become a candidate for the adventure of:

Stage Three: Acceptance

Why is it so hard to wrench ourselves from "could be" and "should be" to Acceptance, or what *is*? The Ladies sometimes call Acceptance the "Al-Anon phase." Al-Anon is the free Twelve-Step program in almost every city where you major in one consummate skill: how to float. It makes little difference in your progress whether an alcoholic is involved, although the program originated for friends and families of alcoholics. In Al-Anon, you try to gentle your immense self-will so that it ceases to gnash its teeth and to try to control other people and events. You begin to accept the existential fact that the world outside yourself is not yours to control. Period. (Hey, what a relief!) You slowly realize how futile it is to try to change another person. FUTILE. The good news is that you get to keep the challenging, fertile job of changing your own behavior and attitudes *and* that you can enjoy yourself in the process. Fertile? They say one does not garden to change the earth, to make it perfect, but to make it more hospitable and more beautiful. So, too, with the garden of love.

Since you can't change the weather, and often you can't even set the sail, why not relax and float down eternity, waving at the attractions — such as all beautiful women? Lighten up and forget being "in charge" of your lover's behavior. You have better things to do — like nuzzling all her good parts. Didn't she come to bring you a sense of wonder?

Once you truly accept, wholeheartedly accept, your lover's flaws, you'll be surprised how nice she can be. Perhaps she's all the things you fell in love with: generous, artistic, funny, sensitive, elegant. Sure, she may also be an indolent hypochondriac, but that is none of *your* business. Take what you need and leave the rest. Ignore that which isn't worth anything anyway. Lady Clitoressa calls love a "blue plate special," a package deal. No substitutions. Accept the reality, for example, that your lover is fun-loving but drinks too much; is artistic but obsessive; is brilliant but a snob. Even your magnificent self-will cannot "cure" her — ever. Do home improvement on the things you can modify, like, say, your own workaholism or rage or denial. Then forgive yourself and forgive her for coping as best we can in this world. Set aside your judgment and feel a little mercy. Roll the pearl of acceptance into your heart of hearts. Imagine what it would be like if you were not called upon to trivialize and embitter your existence by riding herd on someone else's imperfections. Your heart's pearl would bloom like a sunrise.

Once you honestly make the decision to accept love's bitter with her sweet, her disappointments with her joys, her entanglements with her strengths, a lifetime of practice and understanding begins, a path of action. Acceptance is nothing like "resignation," where one passively retreats into martyrdom or abject victimhood, living with the chronic infection of resentment and boredom. Acceptance is, in fact, startling, more like waking up, then actively embracing what is really real, while letting go of all ideas about what "should" be. Lady Clitoressa feels the goal of relationship is not necessarily love, but awakening. Yet how many of us think of wanting someone who loves the truth as well as ourselves? How many of us accept that love encompasses so much of the unlovable?

Stage Four: Commitment

Commitment is a process more than a stage, but usually begins after the women have completed a two- or three-year apprenticeship in the field of couple arts. It dawns when both women begin to work *with* their differences instead of against them. The Ladies call this "refining the fires." It helps immeasurably to keep singing Cris Williamson's song of bravery, "Surrender Dorothy," clear across your sky.

As our great individual egos begin to surrender and stay with each other's differences, a synergistic "we system" is planted, one that can tolerate opposites, dilemmas and paradox. This takes not only acceptance but usually a profound forgiveness, each of which takes time. Forgiveness may mean taking an anger — at our lover, at ourselves, at our family — deeper and deeper until it can diffuse. This brings us to *Lady Clitoressa's Second Law of Relationships: The heaviest work we have to do in relationships is to let go of suffering.* In Commitment, the heart still turns off, but has the ability to open again and again — in fact, to stay somewhat ajar. You discover there are parts of the heart easily opened and those very painful to open. Each woman takes full responsibility for resolving her own inner conflicts, doesn't expect or demand childcare for "her little girl with the broken heart," but can rely on her lover for encouragement. Don't expect instant dramatic change, but progress. Commitment is a slow, gentle and patient process.

The commitment stage is marvelously characterized by the growing proficiency of communication skills. Wishful thinking, mind reading, and absurd, unilateral assumptions begin to be replaced by real exchanges of hopes, attitudes and deepest feelings. We begin to take the risk of saying who we really are and of asking for exactly what we want. There is a new ability to discuss conflicts and resolve them without fear that the sky will fall. Negotiation becomes a social grace as we learn the give and take of compromise, win/win bargaining, and how to just shut up and listen. Two happily "committed" Ladies use the 75 Percent Rule: "We don't attempt to equalize things 50/50. Each one of us instead tries to give in at least

75 percent of the time, do 75 percent of the work, and contribute 75 percent of the energy and expenses. This way, we usually have around 50 percent left over to feel good about."

Honest communication is possible when the relationship has succeeded in creating a root system of mutual trust and stability. The trust is not "I trust you not to displease me," or "I trust you to fix me," but "I trust you to act on your own conscience," and "I trust you to do the best you can to work with me." With such confidence often comes the merging of property and money. Couples may decide to buy a house or to have children. There is ideally a lessening of jealousy and possessiveness, but be sure to keep the reassurances coming. Crystal clear agreements about monogamy/pluralism should have been worked out. Commitment, ironically, is the first stage where an open marriage is even remotely possible, since open marriages must be based on a bedrock of trust. Couples may be more public about their relationship and come out to their family of origin, co-workers and friends. They may even celebrate and honor their commitment in a ritual of union. See the description of such a ritual in the last chapter.

The wonderful, freeing thing about Commitment is how many energy knots it loosens, freeing "us" to be splendidly you and me, to nourish each women's gifts within a stable matrix. Commitment also frees us to learn about, rather than to continually protect, ourselves. We are able to feel safe that no matter how difficult the issue is, this is not "the end." We are more able to step back from the struggle and to examine our real motives and intents. We begin to notice and let go of the various suits of armor we use to shut down: control (get her before she gets me); compliance (predicated on past fears and guilts, not real agreement); indifference and resistance (frozen emotions, sexual passivity, addictions). We can instead pause and ask ourselves, "*Why* does an issue trigger such inner conflict? What am I being asked to learn about myself and my lover? How can we 'break on through to the other side'?"

The danger★ after a few years in Commitment is taking one's partner and the relationship for granted. We forget to celebrate our hard work and blessed good fortune. To avoid relationship rigor mortis, you can continue to transform your love via co-creation:

★ "Considering how dangerous everything is, nothing is really very frightening."
— Gertrude Stein

Stage Five: Co-Creation

"Co-creation" is the term for an evolved relationship state which was coined by therapist Susan Campbell in her excellent book, *The Couple's Journey: Intimacy as a Path of Wholeness*. Many Lesbians have been influenced by this book despite its heterosexual bias. Happily, most relationship skills are transferable, so while Campbell may blank out on Lesbian folkways, she encourages the creative spiritual growth which is a dynamic in all realized Lesbian relationships. Co-creation is the "cup runneth over" tide of love. A world of two is no longer sufficient to contain love energy, and a couple's love flows out as a gift to the world at large. By the Co-creation stage, there is so much trust and harmony that the women are free to create something together beyond the relationship, while being nurtured by it. Women may choose political work such as helping in a battered women's shelter or hospice or sharing various skills with others by presenting workshops. They may decide to raise children, write books or do performance art together.

There are bouquets of closeness and satisfaction which a Co-creative venture can bring to a relationship. It also brings resurrection: a mutual project usually triggers yet another cycle of First Blush, Power Struggle, Acceptance and Commitment. With the new spiral comes new vitality and growth. As you set out on a new path together, you find you didn't marry one woman, you married a cast of multiple personalities — and so did she. "In joining ourselves to one another, we join ourselves to the unknown." Thus *Lady Clitoressa's Third Law of Relationships: Each day you are called upon to learn to love a new person.*

Susan Campbell and many relationship scholars have found that successful, happy long-term relationships, no matter what color on the sexual kaleidoscope, have one quality in common: the concept of the spiritual quest. Both partners, at some level, believe their relationship is a mutual path of awakening, a spiritual journey in growth, self-knowledge and creativity. Each woman understands that her partner is a special guru, a teacher who can mirror back her patterns and conflicts, as well as her sparks of divinity. She acknowledges that relationship power struggles are amazing reflections of her own narrow identity and self-limiting attitudes — if she but dare to look deeply. Lady Clitoressa says that whenever we talk about "the relationship" we are talking about ourselves in another form.

She asks us to list the skills one must learn in order to create a fulfilling relationship and to notice that they are all the skills which promote spiritual growth: daily practice, a sense of destiny or faith in the journey, compassion, patience, ability to transcend difficulty, humor, forgiveness, pursuit of truth. Lesbian partners who both share a common spiritual practice, whether it be Catholic liberation theology or Sufism or Goddess worship, use their spiritual techniques to help them stay open to one another, as well as to provide space and detachment when the going gets rough and sharp edges rend. Co-creation is a supportive, helping dynamic. Its aim is to aid each partner to become the best human being she is capable of becoming.

Perhaps love need not relate to one specific person at all; perhaps it is a quality of character, of heart. A relationship is simply one path to enlightenment — a path not for everyone — but one, like parenting, which makes the spiritual a down-to-earth, here-and-now practice. The Co-creative state of universal love is a journey which never ends, where life is lifted from the ordinary.

Margaret Anderson, the dazzling Lesbian philosopher mentioned previously, was a magnificent "Co-" in the sense of co-creating art within each of her three long-term relationships. Here she speaks of her second great love, the famous singer Georgette Leblanc. Their common spiritual practice was "The Fourth Way" teachings of Gurdjieff.

"I felt at once — as if a prophecy were being made to me — 'There is something perfect in her soul.' For twenty-one years I never saw Georgette Leblanc do anything, never heard her say anything, that did not spring from this perfection. It is a quality, I think, that arises in the creative mind. Putting my trust in this quality, I felt that whatever might be, the best of me (or even the worst) would never be misunderstood by Georgette. It never was. *She always made me feel that there was something perfect in me.* I could never be grateful enough for this distinction. Since she believed it, it must be so. As long as she lived, I felt that I was always smiling."

Writing Love & Partnership Accords

If only the glamorous and urbane dykes of pre-World War II Europe like Margaret Anderson, Lady Troubridge or Janet Flanner had left us copies of their "accords," perhaps we glamorous, urbombed dykes in turn of the century countries would not be so reticent about drawing up personal agreements. Written words of personal commitment can preserve good will and friendship, even sanity herself, which is no mean feat in relationships. Without some sort of "Love & Partnership Accords," a relationship often drifts, taking its form from whatever fate casts its way. This can result in management by crisis, rather than management by the couple's real needs. If you don't understand what each other really needs, you may make decisions by chance and risk hurting one another. Note also that without open agreements, there may be many loaded "secret agreements." ("I expect you to clear your weekend plans with me and I will do the same.") Secret agreements become problems when they are broken, while no one quite understands why they feel so bad.

By written accords, we do not mean legal documents, the ones designed by clever Lesbian lawyers to protect your relationship, health and property from the marauding patriarchy — that is the next section of this chapter. Here we are sounding the trumpets for the homemade written accords you agree to in order to clarify your unique partnership and to protect it from each rascal partner's convenient lapses of memory and unfounded assumptions. These are gentlewomen's agreements, enforceable not in a court of law, only in a court of love. Accords are essentially based on sincerity and good will; without these, accords, no matter how complete or well-conceived, are written in the sand and will never work. Setting unreal goals or pretending compliance sets the relationship up for problems later, which ultimately makes everyone feel angry. Get the best, most honest agreement you can, but don't push for an all or nothing document. Accords are meant to be refined and to grow with you.

Love & Partnership Accords — unlike legal documents — can be simple, romantic, whimsical, poetic, even published in rainbow colors with glitter. There are only a few requirements: they must be clear as a bell, specific as a *haiku*, and built for growth. Accords are perhaps most essential in coping with co-habitation, but can prevent grief even if drafted in early courtship. Accords cannot diminish love; they are, in fact, a tangible way of expressing it. As vows, they can help you to renew your staying power in times of difficulty. But the best reason to draw up Love & Partnership Accords is that the very act itself of sitting down and focusing on the exact means of realizing a happy relationship fosters mutual respect and understanding.

These are the major points usually covered in personal accords:

1. Division of income and property.
2. Ownership of major purchases bought together.
3. Division of household services, maintenance and expenses.
4. Sexual fidelity.
5. Other quality of life considerations such as time and space; holidays; friends and family; co-creative projects; career plans.
6. Children.
7. How to work out disputes.
8. Possible break-up. If you deal with divorce as newlyweds, it won't be such a raving emergency later. Such a consideration may clench your first chakra, but the discussion deals mainly with materialistic issues you can decide rather calmly now since you are far from the eye of any storm.

Each woman should take good time to carefully consider her relationship goals, her negotiables and non-negotiables. The best idea is to create simple, loving accords; don't make them sound like a penal code. They are simply a pledge of happiness with useful forms or guidelines. Would you play tennis without a net? Revise your accords as situations come up that need clarity; don't try to set everything in stone all at once. Be sure to wildly celebrate the signing of your family accords every season. They are the great affirmation that you cared enough to try your very best.

The Sample Love & Partnership Accords
of Tennessee and Wellesley

Because we have so little time before we fly off to eternity, and because we just may pass this way again having to relive everything we didn't learn this time around, we therefore commit ourselves to mutual Evolution in the here-and-now of our Love. We support each other in becoming the best human beings we are capable of becoming. Because we emphatically wish to be together in Exquisite, Laughing and Loving ways, we agree to try to:

1) Be pleasant and convivial, or, if we can't do this, be quiet or mope in our own room until we can be pleasant and convivial.
2) Conduct our lives apart in honorable and peaceful ways that

support our abilities to be fully present for one another when we are together.

3) Stop workaholics at this door, as well as dope fiends and backstairs dames.

4) Set up no new lover involvement which the other is not ready for, nor too often, nor on each other's time. We as primary lovers share prime time: weekends, holidays, birthdays.

5) Tell Tennessee about any affairs Wellesley has on the side. Wellesley, in contrast, expects Tennessee to be profoundly discreet about affairs and to tell her only if she asks.

6) Use our "Code of Fair Fighting" when conflict arises, or walk around the block until we can. Light a candle on the altar in commitment to work through the hard times as creatively and non-violently as we can. If break-up seems threatening, we agree to see a couple counselor before we make any major decisions.

7) Go out of town for a romantic weekend at least once a month.

8) Have a "date night" at least once a week.

9) Protect one another's work time and self-time.

We further agree to try *not* to:

1) Take anything for granted, but learn to clearly communicate our wants, needs and desires.

2) Leave dirty dishes around.

3) Leave a personal trail in any common space.

4) Mess with any business of each other's that does not directly involve us.

5) Bring scarlett wimmen to this house or talk to them on this phone.

6) Nitpick, because we came together to picnic.

We further agree to:

1) Each contribute $500 the first day of each month to the joint food and household expense fund. No exceptions. Exceptions are fined at $10 per day with no exceptions.

2) Not use one another's credit.

3) Tennessee doing most of the marketing, cleaning and gardening because of her remarkably high standards and green thumb. Wellesley doing most of the cooking because of her gourmet tastes. Wellesley further agrees to do the shared accounts and bill paying because she likes numbers and they like her.

4) Acknowledge that each partner has acquired certain property prior to the relationship and each one retains her own property.

5) Keep an inventory of all over $50 purchases and gifts we obtain together.

6) In case of separation, Tennessee keeps our lease and our cats. Wellesley gets the right of first refusal to purchase at market value any of our community held goods or sell them and keep the income — except for art work and sex toys. We will donate these to The Feminist Old People's Home in Milledgeville, Georgia, in remembrance of our once magnificent partnership.

7) The realization that while we don't need to have fun all the time, we will each try to let go of as much suffering as we can.

Signed in celebration, hope and sensuality this fifteenth day of October 1989 by

Jordan Wellesley and _Tennessee Strand_

in love   in love

Where There's a Will...

But where there is not and you die, your biological family can invade your home and strip it bare. To hell with your lover of fifty years. As long as you don't die — being the immortal Lesbian you are — no problem, right? Wrong. If you become hopelessly ill, your family can have you plugged into machines to vegetate, force-fed and abandoned in a nursing home 3,000 miles from your lover and friends. Then, should you be so lucky to die, you can be entombed in a Christian crypt, despite the fact that you always wanted your ashes scattered in your compost pile by your Zen Buddhist buddies. Remember, whoever wrote the *Book of Love* also wrote *The Book of Death*. If you care about your gay relationship, don't leave your loved one in the lurch as well as in deep grief. Any unmarried Lesbian with children who does not have a will is instructed to close this book at once, immediately secure a guardian for the kids and have a lawyer draw up the papers. Otherwise, in case of death or disability, the state may pick a guardian who is an absolute jerk.

108

In the United States, without the force of law behind you in the form of a will and a "Durable Power of Attorney for Health Care," your next of kin or the state will determine what happens to your body in case of total disability, to your estate, to your children, and to your remains. Seventy percent of all people in the United States die "intestate," a word that sounds like it means "without testicles," but means without a will. Many intestates are married and can rely on state statutes to provide for their partner, or they expressly want to place their biological family in the position of making life-and-death decisions, or they simply don't care. Lesbians, obviously, cannot be legally married to reap the built-in protections marriage status conveys. Some of us are estranged from our biological families. Many of us are cheerful anarchists who hate the state meddling in our intimate affairs. Why should we give the state a power in death we never gave it in life? Also remember that the state creams off plenty from your estate in administration fees if you leave no will.

In Lady Clitoressa's Circle alone, two outrageous events occurred because the Lesbians involved did not, as poet Anne Sexton instructed, "build their deaths like carpenters." As one Lesbian lay dying of cancer, her estranged family swept in and banished her lover from the hospice. They seized power of attorney and her father's signature severed the house joint tenancy agreement she had with her lover for eleven years. This allegedly placed the house in tenancy-in-common status, which means at death property share passes by will or to next of kin. When she did die, the parents proceeded to claim title to half the house, to which they had contributed nothing, to which they had never even been invited to dinner. They demanded the lover sell the house and pay them half the proceeds. They could never have tried this if the woman who died had a will and, most importantly, had given someone she trusted power of attorney before she lost consciousness.

In the other case, our Lesbian friend died fully intending, as everyone knew, to leave all her considerable assets to a trust for women artists. Though she had even published a book outlining her vision, she had not set up a legal trust. Unfortunately, after her death, two seedy lawyers moved on the estate, dipping into it for considerable "fees," and tried to use what was left of the money to buy vacation land for themselves. (Yes, they would invite a few artists to party there.) The Lesbian's friends spent a great deal of money and time hiring opposing lawyers to make sure the estate was not further looted, but the matter is still in court three years later. It is unclear if our friend's estate will have anything left after the battle. Meanwhile the lawyers and the state fiddle while women artists starve.

Most Lesbians are aware that so renowned a partnership as

Gertrude Stein and Alice B. Toklas did not escape the homophobia and greed of Stein's relatives. Because even these sophisticated women did not set things up legally, their art fortune, even their apartment, was stripped from Alice when Gertrude died, leaving Alice in complete destitution as well as grief.

The most infamous U.S. case in our own time of a relative's cruelty is, of course, the Sharon Kowalski/Karen Thompson battle. Theirs must also be the greatest love story of the decade. The horrifying tragedy and profound heroism of these two lovers should have every Lesbian rushing to fill out Durable Power of Attorney forms and making wills. Sharon was hit by a drunk driver in 1983, leaving her quadriplegic and brain-damaged. Since then, her partner, Karen, has been locked in a legal battle with Sharon's parents for visitation rights and guardianship. Essentially, Sharon's parents wrote Sharon off as brain-dead, not using the insurance settlement for her rehabilitation. Karen has raised thousands of dollars to do court battle and has tirelessly stumped the country alerting us to what happens if we do not plan for the possibility of disability. Read their story of great courage in *Why Can't Sharon Kowalski Come Home?* by Karen Thompson — and draw up that Durable Power of Attorney for Health Care! There is one included in Thompson's book.

I finally set aside a holiday (holy day) to answer the question: Am I ready to die? Focusing on a "how could I not be among you" scenario is a remarkable and rewarding experience. Life never tastes sweeter. I surveyed my bounty, drew up a will, set up a trust, and got together my Durable Power of Attorney for Health Care. Total cost: $128 because I used self-help law books I borrowed from the library. The very best for us "unmarrieds" are *The Simple Will Book* and *Plan Your Estate*, both by Denis Clifford and both published by Nolo Press with all the requisite forms. Every Lesbian should also read *A Legal Guide for Lesbian and Gay Couples* by Hayden Curry and Denis Clifford, also published by Nolo. After I had drafted things exactly as I wanted them, I hired a smart Lesbian lawyer to review everything, do the fine tuning and explain what I didn't understand. Whatever the cost, think of a will and DPA as insurance policies which pay now in peace of mind and later in dividends of love. Also consider investing in a life insurance policy with your lover as beneficiary. It can buy her the time to reconstruct once mutual economic responsibilities.

When I say "drew up a will," I literally did. My will is illustrated and in color. It even has a few great lines, if I do say so myself. It is immensely satisfying to write your own epitaph and plan your own funeral. I even considered the purchase of a simple but elegant pine coffin ($150) to get some enjoyment out of it in this life (store old love letters?) and use it as a *memento mori* (do not waste time!). A friend bought a plain pine coffin just for its design; it looks great with her Shaker furniture. I opted instead for cremation preceded by organ recycling, about $500 in San Francisco for a no-frills, dignified package. You can even set up a plan for "urnmates." Be careful to shop around. Funeral arrangements in the United States can be the most expensive purchase a consumer makes after a home and a car. Do be sure to send a copy of your will to your next of kin, even if you don't like them very much. Lawyers say most challenges to a will come if its directives take a family by surprise.

Another fine thing to do is to have a party and invite your intended beneficiaries, your executors and powers of attorney people for a gala sort of pre-wake. Ask these friends and family what mementos they would really like; you'll be surprised. You may find yourself now giving away some possessions your friends like a lot better than you do. People will say loving things to you you never dreamed they felt, tell you how much they would miss you, and beg you to take most precious care of yourself forever. You feel bathed in light and almost ready to be gathered to the Mothers.

What Is Remembered Lives

Above all, don't forget to organize your personal papers, letters and memorabilia. They belong in library archives as touchstones of Lesbian civilization. A Great Wicca chant sings, "What Is Remembered, Lives; What Is Remembered, Lives." Remember the validation and pride you felt discovering the Lesbian passion in Emily Dickinson's letters and hidden poetry; the poignant Lesbian longing of Anne Frank (censored from her published *Diary*); the enlightening, loving correspondence between Eleanor Roosevelt and her stomping lover Lorena Hickok (3,360 letters!). Or, go multimedia like Madonna, who we hope saved her tapes of coming out on the David Letterman show.

But for heaven's sake, you don't need to be a celeb. "Everyday" Lesbians' papers, records, audio and video tapes are even more precious to our culture. We are the salt of the earth. There is so much we could have learned from our brave foremothers. Now let your papers and tapes be a mother lode to our daughters. Let us never again allow our history to be obliterated and rewritten by homophobes. No more Sappho in fragments. Even more tragic than censorship is that so much Lesbian history has been lost because no one thought it was important enough to save — this has been true of all women's history. For example, the incredibly rich Lesbian activism of Weimar Germany has been almost totally forgotten. The reason we know so much about the brilliant Lesbian circles of prewar Paris is that photos, correspondence and journals were saved — and labeled! What if they had also made home movies?

Organize things in boxes and keep them away from the enemies of history: dampness and sunlight. Photocopy newsprint because it self-destructs due to the acidic paper. Explicitly date and label EVERYTHING, especially photos, noting who's who — and who's *with* whom for the gossips. What is history anyway but gossip with a long half-life? Use a grease pencil or crayon in labeling backs of photographs. Make sure your Lesbian literary executor understands that you want your papers donated to posterity, exactly as you instruct in your will. Talk to a Lesbian archivist or librarian, our magnificent scholar-witches. They can perhaps help you arrange placement of your papers in a friendly archive. By the way, if you have extra bucks, one of the greatest things you can do is to leave money (now *and* later) to the maintenance of a Lesbian archive in your local area or to a regional or national or international archive.* A funny thing happened to me on the way to the archives: I looked at the books my days are writing, revised several poorly drafted life stories and got moving on some works not in progress . . .

Let us smile with poet Stevie Smith, "Life may be treacherous, but you can always rely on death." True, you cannot cheat death, but if you plan ahead and give her her due, you can have fun with her. Is death not simply another life style? May your bloods then quicken to the stirring refrains of "Co-creation" as the Lesbian Gospel Choir sings:

> *Welcome Lesbians who think you are dead,*
> *Welcome Lesbians who think you are alive,*
> *Welcome hungry ghosts of all realms,*
> *To follow the Light, whatever Light you can.*

---

* See the extensive international listing of women's and Lesbians' libraries and archives in the annual *Directory of Women's Media*, edited by Martha Leslie Allen ($15 from Women's Institute for Freedom of the Press, 3306 Ross Place, NW, Washington, DC 20008); also contact the Lesbian Herstory Archives, Box 1258, New York, NY 10116.

VI.
Fair Fighting:

How to Argue in Peace

HONEY, WHEN ARE YOU going to LEARN: TAKE OUT THE GARBAGE WHEN IT'S FULL! USE THE YELLOW SPONGE FOR THE FLOOR AND THE PINK ONE FOR THE DISHES! DRY YOURSELF OFF IN THE TUB, NOT IN THE BATHROOM! DON'T ANSWER THE PHONE WHEN MY MOTHER CALLS!!!

A nger: be it high decibel, vein-popping drama or silent, tight-jawed fury, we all seem to pay high tax to the grievance collector. The grievance collector is another one of those powerful characters held over from the patriarchy. As Lesbians, we are trying to evolve a less polluting way to deal with anger. The Ladies say fair fighting is worth fighting for, that love is not "war conducted by other means," but love is the other means conducted by peace.

Successful Lesbian couples never, in fact, stop fighting. Why should they? They are two people, not two clones, so of course they will have honestly conflicting needs, opinions and expectations to be negotiated. In successful relationships, however, the partners are elegant fighters, not remedial ones. Elegant fighters come from a place of autonomy, flexibility and compassion, rather than one of shattered egos, desperation and insecurity. They also practice, really *practice*, at fair fighting, understanding that the "School of No Swords" is attained only by pursuing the utmost diligence in fencing exercises. The question is *how* to manage the conflict that will always be with us. Will you drive your partner to the ropes, where, stripped of her dignity, she is declared "at fault," and you "win" (for a while)? Or do you prefer conflict as a cauldron of silently seething resentment where anger is bottled up to poison you like a toxin?

How about a wiser way? Conflict can become discovery in working out a livable, enjoyable path together, as well as a place to get rid of unreal and limiting assumptions, a vessel in which truth can evolve. Lesbians have a tradition of non-violent conflict resolution and activist peacemaking. We intuit that the male way of countering violence with violence leads to hopelessness, and ultimately to death. The War Resisters League, the oldest U.S. anti-war organization, was founded and staffed by Lesbians Jesse Wallace Hughan, Tracy Mygatt and Frances Witherspoon. Lesbian Jane Addams, of Hull House fame, was the first president of The Women's International League of Peace and Freedom. Lesbian writer and activist Barbara Deming has inspired four generations of women to face arrest for civil rights and peace. Lesbians have provided much of the energy and theater in the Pentagon Actions, Seneca Women's

Peace Camp, Mother's Day Anti-Nuke actions, Livermore Weapons Lab protests, etc. If we can fight a murderous system with non-violence and dignity, surely we can fight as cleanly with our lovers. Anger may be innate, but expressing it is learned.

Perhaps it is wise to look at the nature of anger itself. Anger, unlike many difficult emotions such as despair and grief, can be downright energizing. Sometimes nothing but anger can fuel positive change, burning away lies and abuse in its courage and conviction. Anger is as neutral a force as the fire which can heat your house or burn it down. We all need the fire of anger to tell us that something — maybe ourselves — needs fixing. The challenge is to learn to dance with anger, not be consumed by it. See *The Dance of Anger: A Woman's Guide to Changing the Patterns of Intimate Relations* by Harriet Lerner and *Of Course You're Angry: A Family Guide to Dealing with the Emotions of Chemical Dependency* by Gayle Rosellini and Mark Worden. Both books spell out excellent "anger recovery programs." We can all change how anger affects us and learn to express it effectively.

Several of the long-term couples in Lady Clitoressa's Circle are elegant fighters. I noticed that they rarely fight in front of others ("that's not a fight, that's a performance.") When they do, it is clean, usually over as quickly as a summer squall and followed with clear skies above. I wondered if they had some sort of non-aggression pact. "Oh, no," said Harmony, who is one of the most tactful fighters I have ever seen. "We take up the cudgels regularly. We are so different." Harmony went on to explain her *modus operandi*.

"My partner, as you know, is an A.C.A., the adult child of an activist. She is volatile, voluble and actually blossoms in arguments and controversy. She is a smart-mouth, an expert in ridicule and a chess player at logic. She also practices fighting every day as a trial lawyer. To make a point, she freely embroiders facts without compunction. I am a cream puff. I can do none of these things. I hate arguing. My mind blanks, my palms perspire and I yearn to be a thousand miles away on a calm lake. Like many women, I was taught to be subtle and vague, and that my role was to be nurturing and non-needful myself. So when our conflicts first arose, I gave in, I gave up, I sobbed, I sulked, I stuffed a million grievances. I did everything to end all conflict forever. In the process of trying to duck anger, my ego was devastated. My lover's was hardly scathed.

"I finally realized this way was nutso. I couldn't hold back the conflict which naturally arose. It also dawned on me I couldn't win against my beautiful samurai — but that I didn't have to *lose* either. All I needed to do was to stay present and learn and keep fighting as cleanly as I could. The idea is not to win, but to aim carefully. I realized she didn't have such a mighty sword; I just gave her one with my irrational dread of anger and power. Once I got over the idea that I had to 'win' something, I started loosening up. I began picking up some techniques on how not to be a victim and how to keep my calm, my self-respect, and usually get what I need. Here is a grab bag of what works for me.

"First of all, I recognize some things are too important to fight about. Number one is religion. Curb your dogma — or furious non-dogma. Everyone has a right to her own spiritual life, for Goddess' sake. Number two is having kids. Here compromise is impossible — half a kid? Finally, the futile old battle-ax of monogamy/pluralism is an energy-sink of black hole proportions. Love and let love.

"Fight about everything else, especially 'little things' if they might build up and fester. Make it enjoyable. Duel in the sun. Never 'stuff' anger. Stuffing makes you crazy and oblivious to all your partner's wonderful qualities like how sweet she was when your dog ate her legal briefs. None of my relationships ever perished under big blows: they were whittled away by resentment after resentment. It is said that a thousand gnat bites can be fatal, or, as Edna St. Vincent Millay put it, 'It's not love's going that hurts my days/But that it went in little ways.' I try to remember *Lady Clitoressa's Law of Surface Tension: There is no such thing as unexpressed anger.* If you do not let anger out openly and discharge it, you go passive-aggressive, 'forgetting' things, being late; or you emote tension; or you feel boredom (a kind of hostility without energy); or you withdraw sexually. Some kind of inner intelligence always wants to express anger. Then, an even deeper intelligence needs to design exactly *how* we express this anger in order to get what we need. When anger is squandered in gutter language and lousy syntax, nothing changes except that the hostility escalates.

"For me, a great technique is never to react to rhetorical statements, which are the mainstay of big league arguers like my lover. Rhetorical statements are dramatic, if empty, exclamations like, 'You *do* know how to break an egg, don't you?!' when I splattered one all over her shoe. All sarcasm, all exaggeration and most analogies are simple rhetoric. 'You sound just like Phyllis Schlafly.' 'Your idea would be about as intelligent as putting pennies in the fuse box.' If you waste time reacting to rhetoric, you'll never get to the real issue. Rhetoric is designed to needle you; don't let it. Merely smile a disarming half-smile because you know the true secret of rhetoric. She will think you appreciate her attempt at wit. Stay with the issue or dismiss the whole thing as trivial.

"Along with recognizing rhetoric for what it is, try to keep in mind the difference between opinions, facts and truth when you argue or listen. We tend to believe everything we ourselves hold is the truth; at best, it may be a facet of the truth. Most so-called truths are actually emotional opinions and are about as reliable as a lie."

I asked the Ladies for some other words to the wise. They came up with words to the unwise in "Statements Never to Stoop To" below. Make your own list and honor it assiduously. We all know irrevocable statements we should never make to our lover, ones that scar a soul. "You've not been able to sell one piece of your schlock sculpture, and you never will." These sort of statements are nuclear bombs, unthinkable to use. Many "no wonder" statements are irrevocables. "No wonder everyone leaves you." "No wonder your whole family laughs at you." Here is a sample list of megaton statements to freeze in verbal disarmament.

Ten Statements Never To Stoop To

1) You act just like a man.

2) Can't you ever do anything right?

3) You have disgusted me ever since [some fatal blow of the century], and you always will.

4) Just don't be here when I get home. Slam! [Never walk out without setting an approximate time of return, or you're like a poor loser who throws down her tennis racket and stalks off the court.]

5) I never really loved you.

6) If you ever really loved me . . . [snivel].

7) After all I've done for you . . . [another snivel].

8) Statements which begin, "You never . . . "

9) Statements which begin, "You always . . . " ["Never" and "always" are usually lies; worse, they render someone so defensive they close down.]

10) Why don't we just break up?

One Strike and You're Out (Battering)

Physical violence is a one-way ticket out of all Lesbian relationships. Period. Violence is never an acceptable way to deal with anger. Studies show there is some incidence of Lesbian battering. The only difference between it and heterosexual battering is that there is less of it and there are fewer services for Lesbian battered and batterers. Lesbians also tend to get out of such relationships faster than women do with violent men. Still, Lesbian battering will exist as long as there are Lesbians with poor anger/impulse control who learned patterns of family violence and who have Lesbian partners with low self-esteem. If you do experience battering, end the relationship. This is the only action a batterer understands. A cycle of violence always escalates, despite grandiose apologies and promises.*

Famous Misunderstandings

One erection of the ego — and pow! — a Famous Misunderstanding is in the making. Our ego literally "takes" offense, choosing to pick up a burden to fuss and worry over. We could be singing in the shower, learning calligraphy or designing a free food program, but no. We have opened an offense gymnasium where we lift great weights. Here we take our partner's inventory and select the improvement exercise program for her. This handily leaves no time for us to work on changing ourselves. But guess what? The only person you can change is yourself. Your partner is going to change at her own pace or remain pretty much the same. You are going to have to live with her process and her limitations. Not until you wholeheartedly let go and accept her as she is, then, and only maybe then, will some mutual change occur by psychic osmosis. But don't count on it.

---

* For Lesbian battering counsel, call the twenty-four-hour hotline of W.O.M.A.N. in San Francisco (415) 864-4722, or call the hotline of the National Coalition Against Domestic Violence, 1-800-333-SAFE, for local referral to Lesbian-supportive services. See also *Naming the Violence: Speaking Out About Lesbian Battering* edited by Kerry Lobel (Seal Press, 1986).

Personal Habits and Housekeepry

Take, for example, well, take offense at her *déclassés* personal habits and housekeepry. These create Famous Misunderstandings of shocking magnitude. Your beloved is as oblivious of the toothbrush dots she sprays all over the mirror as she is to the compost pile she leaves in the kitchen sink drainbasket. Her hairbrush looks like a rodent's dream house. She refuses to practice the healthful intricacies of the kitchen "dual sponge system" (one sponge for floor, one for above), as well as several intelligent, efficient procedures you have advanced over the years. Wake up and smell the java. She may never change. Why waste an iota of time and energy making two lives miserable over housekeepry? Drop your nagging, prickling irritation and substitute benign cynicism. Why be a disgruntled purist when you could be a cheerful one? Spend a fraction of what you would in irritation energy and maintain top cleaning standards for both of you. Write this off as your contribution to environmental aesthetics.

Life is too short and too precious to waste it running a personal habits police department. "But," you ask, "is it *fair* that I always take out the kitty litter?" Well, do you hate the cats as much as you do your lover when they do not do their share? No. You remember their sweetness in other ways, that they love you even if they can't (won't) hold to your standards of correct living. In these cases, you will know peace only when you resolve your answer to Lady Clitoressa's query, "Do you want to be happy or do you want to be fair?" Happy, of course. Life is not fair. So, you alone clean out the litter in sixty seconds flat, glad that your cat's asshole works better than your lover's nose. Now you can cheerfully move on with your life. In housekeepry, as in spiritual matters, a partnership usually lives off the capital of the more evolved. Fair, yes?

Money

How about Famous Misunderstandings over money? First of all, never loan your beloved any amount of money you would not give her as a gift. Never. *Voilà*, most of your money misunderstandings are solved. Next, be open to fully discussing money in the relationship simply because money is a vast mysterious force affecting your whole existence whether you want it to or not. Money is a deep symbolic projection in every Western psyche, whether looked upon as a powerful form of energy or as the toilet tissue of an economy gone haywire. If you and your lover have been traveling in a different social class, expect some turbulence ahead for you both in

120

the interclass cabin. Women raised in a privileged class, who have never known real poverty, rarely understand the extreme "scarcity mentality" that many other women are taught. Most women, however, internalize an economics of relative scarcity. After all, women own less than one percent of the earth's property and only ten percent of its income, according to the United Nations statistics. With the stakes so skewed, no wonder women "worry" about money, and two of us together can be downright anxious.

Lesbians do not, however, equate money with self-worth and power to the degree this is done in hetero and gay male relationships, *American Couples* reports. Gertrude Stein's "I always wanted to be rich, but I never wanted to do what you have to do to become rich," remains true for many Lesbians. Like Gertrude, of course, we appreciate our passionate perks. Lesbian are, however, deeply concerned with being financially independent, but the partner who is wealthier is unlikely to be considered "dominant," as is true among hets and gay males. Still, Lesbians do fight over money, especially when we both are poor and become stressed when there are little resources to tide us over in emergencies. Tabloids to the contrary, rich people as a class divorce less often than poorer folk, probably due to less money stress and more tax advantages.

The best way to avoid Famous Misunderstandings over money is to be frank about your personal money belief system, one based on emotion and family of origin. "It's un–American not to live on credit." "I'm never happy spending money unless I get a bargain." "The money always turns up." "I'm terrified when my savings account is low." If you and your partner's money belief systems are totally incompatible (the cup is half full vs. the cup is half empty), keep separate accounts, mind your own business and stay tolerant. A couple recognized that one woman was much better at budgeting and one was much better at spending. They each stretched a little and now enjoy their money more. Many Lesbian couples have a "three pot" system for money: each woman holds her own separate, discretionary account and contributes to a third account for common purchases. Whereas het law enables married couples to instantly commingle all finances and consider it "commonwealth," it usually takes years of trust for Lesbians to make this move.

Space Wars: Intimacy/Distance

Let us continue with Famous Misunderstandings. How about "Space Wars"? Here Aurelia wants acres of separate space and time just when Billie needs more and more closeness. One prevailing theory holds that Billie is overfunctioning by expressing all the need and clinging for both partners. Aurelia gets to avoid confronting her own need and insecurity because Billie is so loud. Space Wars has an absolutely loaded sexual component to escalate excitement. Billie is seemingly afire with lust. Aurelia is too busy, too tired, too anxious, too bored, or too damn something to indulge. Then Billie gets too pushy and Aurelia becomes even more entrenched in her need for space, not sex. We all know, however, it takes two women not to have sex together, so it usually turns out that both Aurelia and Billie are getting kicks out of no sex. Lesbian therapists call this strange phenomenon "Lesbian Bed Death," or LBD. LBD usually occurs after the First Blush relationship stage, during Power Struggle. LBD is generally one part boredom and one part unresolved conflict, with a dash of internalized homophobia thrown in.

The boredom is easiest to solve because all that takes is simple behavior modification and willingness to act sexy even if you don't initially feel hot. Such play-acting is, after all, for a good cause — and don't we effortlessly spend much of the day acting one way when we feel another? Do you think your therapist is really interested in your old LBD, or just acts fascinated?

So tart up your technique with sex toys, hot videos and erotic writings, fantasies, and new scenery. Sit on the kitchen counter wearing a merry widow and invite your lover for *hors d'oeuvres*. Why not hire *à trois*, as in *ménage*? If this is too scary, hire "house call" masseuses for a half-hour to relax your bodies into that warm-honey-laced-with-spice state. Then roll around all slithery with your girl banking those fires. Make a regular "date" with your lover, just like the old days. Set aside a time; make sure it is private and uncluttered. Don't fall for that fallacy that if it is not spontaneous, it is not sexy. Lots of "spontaneous" sex is a dud, as we all know. What are more choreographed than First Blush dates? You know every move by heart and you love it: exactly when she is arriving, where you'll go for dinner, that you'll take her hand in the movie, she'll kiss you in the car, that you'll ask her in . . . We make dates for every other important event; why not sex?

Make love in semi-risky places. Try fast sex, like five- or ten-minute sprints. Try expressly *not* to go "all the way" for a week, for a month. You'll find you are both smoking in good old celibacy. Be encouraging whenever she does make love with you. Tell her everything she does that you like. Ask her, "How can I make it better for you?" and she'll probably ask the same of you. Give phone sex. Try committing one act every season that you said you would *never* do (just to inform your biases). Court your lady like a queen, but do not demand — or expect — genital sex if a Famous Misunderstanding is in the healing. Go for "outercourse," everything from intimate conversation to outrageous flirting to soft-core cuddling. Intercourse can be pretty much tunnel vision anyway. Graze all over her with warm poetry, bide your time and enjoy yourself. Ask her to hold you while you masturbate if you can't wait. Throughout all, observe *Lady Clitoressa's Fourth Law of Motion: If you do not try too hard, it gets hard all by itself.*

Fusion/Fission

The final Famous Misunderstanding said to cause Lesbian relationship havoc is really many misunderstandings, all the ones which cluster around what couple counselors dub the "Lesbian Fusion Syndrome." (Do Lesbians without therapists have any of these problems?) Fusion seems to be one of those situations where anything pushed too far becomes its opposite, as in the yin/yang swirl. Lesbians have the capacity to become so close emotionally and physically that we can "fuse" in an almost primal intimacy. Remember primal intimacy — that warm, delicious sense of mother/child love/empathy which radiates safety, nurturance and bliss? Add Lesbian eroticism to this heady brew and you create a mixture of colossal intoxication. So who cares? What is wrong with the urge to merge, if it feels so good?

The problem is you decide you'll try to stay in fusion all the time. You go to any lengths with your lover to avoid the bouts of splendid isolation which you have forgotten are also a source of strength and delight. You bury differences. You begin to "lose" yourself in the relationship. Panic and resentment set in, finally leading to — well, fission. Another couple done gone. While all humans have a primal need to bask in empathetic closeness, we also have a primal need for individuation and boundaries. A healthily functioning psyche must sometimes stand against an empty sky to achieve and appreciate her own unique being.

The trick is to move gracefully in and out of the contrasting states of fusion/fission, clinging to neither one. Accept *Lady Clitoressa's Fifth Law of Motion: Fusion leads to fission and back again.* In a couple where each person holds the powerful, innate feminine ability to affiliate, empathize and nurture, the blazing intimacy created can begin to take on a life of its own, dimming individuality in its zenith. "Who shall we be today, you or me?" It has been said that heterosexuals operate in an energy field of centrifugal force and gays in one of centripetal force. Our destiny is to learn to balance dynamic, merging energy. Our fusion, in many ways so desirable, so

123

marvelously deep, may get out of harmony. Fusion can go fascist when it perceives any separation or difference as a danger. Fascist fusion sees the naturally changing cycles of closeness and distance as loss, not as renewal.

A symptom of fusion tyranny occurs in the Lesbian couple in which each partner does not have her own separate friends. The couple may have no friends at all and isolate "us against the world." Lesbians who cannot seem to spend any leisure time separately or maintain independent interests are probably in fusion. Another symptom is likely to be raging co-dependency. "I need you to tell me who I am." One woman internalizes the other's problems and pain. Other addictive behavior is common: control issues, denial, substance abuse. Mother/child dependency roles may occur which bring up incest taboos. In any event, suffocation by fusion naturally leads to diminished sexual desire and is a leading factor in LBD. Where is the romantic mystery as we become the same, when there are no surprises by "the other" in which to delight?

Fusion ultimately begins to collapse of its own boring intensity. Enter fission. Fission may take the guise of another woman, recruited to "prove" one partner's independence. It may come in the form of constant bickering to exhibit at least superficial differences and control needs. A woman may exhibit so much pain over her "lost" self she will use almost any pretext to back out of the relationship. Once we understand the amazing dynamic of fusion gone fascist, we can create non-lethal fissions to balance fusion power. This way we can appreciate moments of merging, a state everyone dreams of, while remembering that fusion is a creature of the tides. She comes in and departs, leaving an empty beach of possibility. Don't panic. In a "touch and go" world, touch returns. Individuation need not mean abandonment, nor merging mean engulfment.

Carefully nurture your sense of self — to create a real individual there to be touched. Many Lesbians feel that meditation or another daily spiritual practice helps to keep the heart open as well as to forge clear, honest boundaries of the self. Spiritual practice also provides a healing space for wounds and raggedy edges. Keep your own special family of friends. Pursue separate interests. These make you more interesting to the other (and to yourself). Maintain private, alone space, even launch a "private evening" out every week or so, one in which you need never discuss what you did. Rather than bicker over safe, pseudo- or trivial differences, confront and negotiate real differences as they come up over class/race background, money, politics, aesthetics. Don't be afraid of clean anger and challenging conflict as long as you keep:

The Code of Lesbian Civility

The evolved Lesbian holds a code of civility almost unknown in our surly patriarchy of abuse and ultra-violence. Lesbians are one of the few classes on earth who still believe in *noblesse oblige*, the beauty of good manners and consideration. Manners are never to be confused with etiquette — etiquette being confusing in itself with its silly rules designed to keep the caste system alive. Rules of etiquette make life more difficult, not more pleasurable, since they perpetrate a system of hypocrisy devised to cultivate class warfare and humiliation. Etiquette rules are found in the heartless formalities of the upper class as well as, ironically, in the conformities of s & m ritual and in teenage gang behavior. Most Lesbians blithely ignore false etiquette — for example, that the oyster fork is on the far right. We simply use our fingers or mouth to place the morsel in our lover's lips. Such convivial, kindly intention is the stuff of which manners are made. Manners reveal one's hopes, standards and strivings. Manners are inclusive, not exclusive. If etiquette is comparable to theology, manners are morality. They have conscience and soul. They improve the quality of existence.

It is no wonder most Lesbians are adept at manners and uncommon decency. Women have always been the torch-bearers of manners, heading the various "schools" of each era. Lord Chesterfield is a fluke, but he does not count because his advice is snotty one-upmanship and misogynist to boot. The lavender lord, Quentin Crisp, one of the stately homos of England, does dispense manners advice in the *grande dame* tradition. Totally unconcerned with the petit point of etiquette, he beautifully demonstrates that "manners are love in a cool climate," as he wrote in *Manners from Heaven*. The great dames of manners are famous Lesbian *salonnières* like Madame de Staël ("Love is the whole history of woman's life; it is but an episode in a man's") and, of course, Natalie Barney. Then there are Fanny Fern, Dorothea Dix, Emily Post, Eleanor Roosevelt (yes, she wrote hundreds of columns on manners), Amy Vanderbilt, and the inimitable Miss Manners. Guess who the Lesbians are here?

Good manners are more than diplomatic cologne. They demand nerves of steel and hearts of gold. Life is full of irritations and social mutants. It is not easy to deal non-violently with intrusive, abusive and downright disgusting people. Since Lesbians have virtually no cut-throat role models or abusive social structures and forms of our own, we naturally depart from the social behavior of the pit bull society we find ourselves in. Thus, the Ladies' adherence to good manners makes them at least seem on the outside what they ought to be on the inside. It is well known, of course, that the more polite you act, the more polite you become, as in "the more you come, the more you can." Note good manners always take precedence over bad. In social situations you bring either darkness or light. How do you follow the light, not only if provoked by some dickhead, but if slandered by your own true love? By not reacting to calumny in kind, thereby refusing to create more abuse pollution and allowing your slanderer to set the level. As Lillian Hellman said, "You lose your manners and you're poor."

Depending on the nature of the remark aimed at you, diffuse it with, "You could be right about that," or "How *very kind* of you to mention it," or with a total non sequitur, "Where do the stars go when they die?" Admittedly, it is hard to resist responding to the boys' taunt, "What are you, a Lesbian?" with "If you are the alternative." Or to "Don't you ever wear a dress, dyke?" with "Not in your size." Or to the old, "Which one of you is the man?" with "I'm too much woman for you and more of a man than you will ever be."

If you are audience to a homophobic, sexist, racist, or ageist joke, ask in a loud, shocked tone, "Do you think *that* is funny?" Repeat several times. Never be embarrassed to sound like a broken record to someone who is pushing for a fight. If you repeat ten times, "I prefer to change the subject," you win. To every kind of attack on you resembling, "That is the dumbest excuse I ever heard," keep calmly repeating your decision. Don't fall into the trap of giving sensible reasons for it. Reasons give your arguer something to argue about. Compare the turmoil level of conversations #1 and #2:

(1)	(2)
"Why won't you do it?"	"Why won't you do it?"
"Because I don't have time."	"Because I can't?"
"What if you stayed just a little later?"	"Why not?"
	"Because I can't possibly."
"Because I have to cook dinner."	"Why not?"
"Why don't you let X cook?"	"Because I can't, even though I love you madly."
"Because she's expecting me to."	[End of wrangling.]
"Well, why do you always care more what she wants than what I do?"	
[Wrangling *ad infinitum* . . .]	

Do we really want to live without the drama of wrangling in favor of calm manners? Lady Clitoressa does not believe relationships are ruined by complex things like fusion or finances or intimacy thresholds. She says that the problem is that loving people who were once gallant and considerate allow themselves to become fault-finding emotionaholics. "Why can't we just look upon 'faults' as 'eccentricities'? Why rudely impose our mercurial moods upon another rather than let go of them privately? Why is it acceptable, for example, to allow a beeper to go off in bed for every neurosis and emotional scar? Lovers once left their muddy boots and moods outside the bedroom door."

Can Anyone Hear Me?

To most angry outbursts from strangers, the correct response is usually no response at all, except Harmony's above mentioned half-smile or some judo remark like the tar-baby, "You could be right about that." Ova and out. In the case of anger from your significant other, leading studies have shown that the hardest response is also the wisest: listen to her. Just listen. Why do we instantly drop everything when attacked to brew up our own reactive stew of hurt, anger and fear? Just listen. This is a challenge of colossal proportions because our instinct is to shut down, react crossly or violently, or try to hush everything up in premature capitulation. What the outraged party usually wants, amazingly enough, is to be able to emote without interruption and feel that her pain has been heard, acknowledged and registered. You can never "solve" her anger; she must. When she has had her say, you can ask her specifically what she would like you to do to help. Often this is not apparent in the heat of battle.

Most women will be flabbergasted to get a focused hearing with a truly open-ended response. Communication analysts say that most of the time we are talking to ourselves. Nobody is really listening. Humans are capable of hearing 400 to 600 words per minute, whereas people speak around 120 words per minute. Ask yourself how you use all the processing intervals when someone is speaking to you. If you are not interrupting them, you are probably chattering away to yourself, preparing a rejoinder, praying for surcease, or daydreaming.

Remember how you could listen so radiantly to your love during courtship? How you heard all the themes and subthemes? Try to

127

regain the same sensitivity. Here are additional aids because while we hear every whisper of adoration, it takes every listening technique in the world to stay tuned to anger or criticism. First, sit down if possible or at least plant your feet firmly on the ground. This keeps you from being blown away. Suck a cheek in or keep one full of tongue. This prevents you from interrupting. Open your hands. Whenever possible, run a mellow thought through your loom: remember how she took care of you like an angel when you lost your job, got evicted and were audited by the I.R.S., all in one week? At least this is not that bad. Try to take all criticism as a free pass leading to self-evaluation. You are likewise free to totally reject unfair, immaterial or mean-minded words.

Still, listening is hard because of a welter of our own feelings is released as soon as someone tries to convey theirs. Work to hear your lover's feelings as *her* feelings, ones she has a right to experience. They are not usually the whole truth or the whole picture, so don't judge them that way. Sheath your critical intelligence for the moment. Watch what she is feeling. Deaf people often "hear" better than others because they are watching the body language which communication experts say is more explicit than word content or tone. Even if your lover's facts are all "wrong," here is an experience in search of a telling. Again, remember the power of the wordless message. All this may require a degree in therapy or a priesthood in egoless Buddhahood, but do the best you can for the longest period. All the Twelve-Step programs are "listening tanks," which accounts for much of their success. Go to one of these to practice, and you will become skillful at waiting thirty seconds before you interrupt someone. Then say almost anything gently except, "Thank you for sharing that with me," which deserves obliteration.

Lady Clitoressa said that once in the still of the night she was in entrancement with her cat Burma Burmese. Burma Burmese distinctly spoke these words: "It is not that we do not talk; people do not listen."

Fair Fighting Guidelines

By now it should be obvious that if you have the self-discipline to allow your lover to speak her piece and the magnanimous self-esteem of good manners, most of your fighting days are over. Still, there are naturally going to be sticky conflicts to resolve, emotional bulls in your china shop, personal fouls, and general *sisterhood interruptus* to deal with. Great fighters, like great artists and lovers, develop a skillful technique to improvise upon. Before a Fair Fighting system can work, each woman must also share a common vision of conflict. First, it is essential to believe that it is vital and functional to have and share anger along with good will and a commitment to change. There should be a pursuit of truth, while eschewing lies, secrets and games. It must be accorded that each woman has the right to her needs, conditions and sensitivities, a sort of "I'm O.K., You're O.K." affirmation. It must likewise be accorded that all such rights also entail responsibility to self, our partners and the relationship. Finally, it must be agreed that all power and authority are to be as equal as possible, that the whole point is cooperation, not power plays and competition.

The general flow of an opener to a Fair Fight bout can be summarized in the following formula: "When you [*describe action*], I feel [*describe feeling*] and then [*describe impact of behavior on life*]. I want you to do [*action*] because of [*purpose*]." Example: "I feel resentful when you leave your clothes and dirty dishes all over the common areas of the house for days. I feel like I am your maid picking up everything. I want the house to be cleared up every week, and I don't want to do it alone any more."

Elegant fighters will note the aggrieved party "owns," takes responsibility for, her feelings about the problem with clear "I" statements. She does not impugn her partner's character with moral blame or name calling, the instant route to non-cooperation. She does not make extraneous judgments or psychological diagnosis. She treats one issue at a time. In contrast, here is an opener with nowhere to go but down. "You are a slob. If you had any consideration, you wouldn't treat common space like your pigpen room and car. You think everyone loves being your personal slave. I, for one, am sick of being told I can't smoke in the house I clean and take care of."

Nor does an elegant fighter ever "ambush" her partner. This is picking a fight when someone has just come home from a long day's work or is in the middle of a busy or trying situation. Before criticizing anyone, it is always wise to assess whether both of you are in a good frame of mind. If the conflict is a major one, it is best to tell your partner you have a problem and arrange a special time with her to discuss it. Elegant fighters never, of course, fight when they could be sleeping or making love.

Steps in Negotiation

Go slow, above all, go slow. In argumentative haste, there is much folly and sputtering. We tend to see people as the problem, not the patterns which actually are. If you are the recipient of anger, review listening poses for temporary relief: place feet on the ground, insert tongue in cheek, and relax lower chakras, especially the abdomen where the great *hara* resides. Then LISTEN. If you begin to become overwhelmed by your attacker's anger, rush from the room assuring her you will be right back after you consult the *I Ching* for a moment. This act provides you calm breathing space, and the *I Ching* actually does bring a lot of perspective to hot issues. It is full of "No Blame" and "No Judgment" prompters. If you are not an *I Ching* aficionado, light a candle for calmness. Then come back and LISTEN. Whenever you can, put yourself in her place, showing your magnificent elasticity and your remarkable gift in the "willing suspension of disbelief" we all learned in theater arts. Then give in. Yes. Life is too short to grapple with petty rebukes. It helps to remember at least three good qualities this woman has at her best. Kiss her cheek, go forth and try to err no more.

Some issues, however, are not petty. Suppose you both have what can only be described as a sizzler of rage, pain and mistrust to get through. Here try to follow the following twelve not-so-easy steps. The more volatile things are, the more important it is to have a structure like this. Set aside special quiet time to discuss the problem, but don't wait too long or things will fester.

Guidelines For Peace

1) Create "I" contact and clarity. Before you meet, take some time alone to understand what you are feeling and why. Focus your goals so you can keep on track when the going gets tough.

2) Set a time limit from five to thirty minutes. If you don't get anywhere, negotiate for more time or set another meeting. A time limit reinforces a focus rather than meandering. It also prevents "wear down" tactics.

3) Begin with compliments and affirmation. You can always, no matter how disaffected, say you appreciate being with a woman generously open and committed to positive conflict resolution. Then define the exact issue, and define it as shared, as *we* do not agree, as *our* problem, not as an exercise in raking over someone's faults.

4) Say precisely what happened, what the other person did. Isolate components, and stay in the here and now. Forget old wars or you'll never wind down the current one.

5) Say what the action did to you, your ego position. This can be quite vulnerable, but really clarifies a solution. Try to state your position as a fear you would be delighted to give up. This is more likely to make your partner helpful, rather than defensive. "When you come home late and don't call me, I'm afraid you're hurt or are with another woman." NOT "I feel discounted when you are late." The latter, besides being vague, masks as an "I" statement, but actually makes a psychological interpretation, setting up defensiveness. Ditto, "I feel misunderstood," and "feel rejected," which sound sniveling and futile.

6) Then LISTEN — with all the attention and egolessness you can muster. Don't interrupt except for essential clarification. Exchange of information may go back and forth for quite some time.

7) Finally comes the pitch for change. Ask for 100 percent of what you want; you can negotiate later, but maybe you won't have to. Don't go into all the things you don't want; this usually deteriorates into the blame game. "I want you to call me as soon as you know you'll be late. Then I won't worry and can plan my own evening." State your position as a want, not a demand.

8) Now you've reached the negotiation stage and — hey! you're still speaking. Brainstorm to settle for what everyone needs. "You can't always get what you want . . . " as the song goes. Don't hold out for total agreement or for an apology with bells on. Accept what's reasonable, not perfect. Quit while you're ahead.

9) Use a thirty-minute cooling-off period if the negotiation is a tough one, as in the following polarity: "I don't want you to date Lesbians you work with because I never feel safe since you see them every day. Plus I never know when you're working or if you are just fooling around," versus the other's "If I can't have a drink or go to a movie with a co-worker at night, I feel bound and gagged."

10) Again, if the conflict is a thorny one, write out the solution and its process of implementation. Even the most honest people seem to filter information and remember only what they want to. If the solution doesn't work, even when it is quite clear what was agreed to, something is awry, and it's back to the bargaining table. When your partner regularly agrees to one thing but never implements her part of the bargain, she is an infantile model who should perhaps be traded in for a responsible adult.

11) Real pros with detachment and confidence evaluate how they fought and how to improve. Each woman rates herself on below-the-belt tactics, here and now focus, specificity, humor, and

her response-ability. The fight itself can be rated according to its resulting increase or decrease of hurt, information, fear, trust, reparations, catharsis, affection.

12) Always end with affirmative closure. Thank each other for trying and for compromises made; go for saving her face and acting with grace. This does not mean you have to slavishly apologize or agree to any idiocy you've been subjected to in the heat of battle, but do forget that "one last word." Kiss her instead. It is wise to recognize that people heal differently after a fight. One woman may need lots of continuing reassurance; another may want hours of time alone.

If these dozen steps seem terribly difficult to follow during high emotional storms, don't worry. Be patient and try to hold to them as well as you can. They become internalized and easier to practice with time. Change is slow, but setbacks do not mean failure.

It is also helpful to touch each other during the process. People are used to feeling competitive and alienated during conflict, whereas they could feel intimate and cooperative. Resolution of a conflict is, after all, in each woman's self-interest and strengthens the relationship. Helen Colton in *The Gift of Touch* found when a person is touched that more hemoglobin is released into the blood, refreshing one with oxygen. She also notes European friends touch each other about one hundred times an hour, Americans rarely more than three or four times. Colton's studies show a correlation between the degree of violence/cruelty and touching within thirty cultures: the less touching, the more violence.

Forgiving

Lesbians seem to have a fondness for Reinhold Niebuhr's "Serenity Prayer": *Grant me the serenity to accept the things I cannot change, the courage to change the things I can, and the wisdom to know the difference.* If we could live this prayer plus add one more magnanimous pledge line, a line on being granted the generosity to forgive, we would surely be healed in this life. Let's face it: many conflicts cannot be "resolved." There are some deeds so hurtful, so beyond reparation, it seems that they must live in infamy. But why give them the power of life, living and reliving what has passed? Do we heal or do we keep the wound open? Forgiveness is a kind of power, the fresh air, the water, the light which grants us the freedom to heal, to begin again, to love. If blaming is one of the most futile or human actions, forgiveness is one of the most profound. Forgiveness does not mean we have to trust and allow a nogoodnik back into our life. It is said to err is human, to forgive divine, to forget foolhardy. But we can let the outrage go.

Vedanta holds there is no sin, only ignorance. The Twelve-Step program says some of us are sicker than others; reality says everyone makes mistakes. Christianity is, as usual, full of contradictions, but Jesus probably said, "Judge not that ye may not be judged." Since Buddhists consider us all manifestations of the One, the wrongdoer is simply a version of ourselves, perhaps our shadow. We require, for example, a non-ethical person to define our own morality. Modern psychology seems to back up this "shadow principle." Notice the more you hate someone, the more you fear their perceived dark quality in yourself. Who is more homophobic than a latent homosexual, more obsessed with sexuality than a puritan?

Forgiveness, like fair fighting, is an acquired skill for most of us, a slow and gentle exercise of the heart. The Ladies advise beginning with your physical body. Take your anger deep and deeper until you feel it where you carry it, in your neck, shoulders, belly, your heart, into your very cells. You probably can't release anger until you have taken it to its primordial vibrancy or pain. You may have to let your heart be open even to being closed for a while. (Note that mere vengeance does not really touch the source of the pain and also that in vindictiveness we usually feel so small.) Finally, you will go as far as you can with your pain. You will cross the finish line and utterly collapse. You are now empty. You can forgive yourself for all the pain, for whatever your part in it actually is. You are now on your way to forgiving the other. You are no longer being lacerated with her monkey on your back. You have gone the distance; you don't have anything more to prove. You are ready to begin something new.

We close our minds and live in bitterness for such petty reasons. Compare the ability to forgive in the context of rape, incest, torture, premeditated killing and war. These things unwind a normal mind. In less threatening situations, we too can surely go to our hearts, refuse to turn against ourselves, and rearrange the components like a Frida Kahlo painting where:

*the roots of a tree are coming out of a skeleton buried in its soil
death fertilizing life*

as this rape nourishes my understanding
and suffering teaches our souls.

— Judith Ragir

The Hebrew word for compassion, *rachamin*, literally means womb, a new birth, a new start. "Let what was, be gone; what will be, come; what is now, be."

VII.
Fifty Ways
to Leave
Your Lover

Fifty? There is, as every wise Lesbian knows, one and only one way to leave your lover: with her laughing, blowing you a kiss. If you cannot pull this off — becoming behavior in unbecoming a couple being as rare as silk pajamas — do not leave your lover at all. Let her leave you. This is much easier. Gently admit to whatever accused of or adopt a serious character deficiency. Then sadly bow out. ("Yes, I am selfish and obstinate." "Yes, I am a workaholic." "No, I cannot be sexually faithful in this life.") Shut the door softly, firmly, but like Cole Porter's Miss Otis send your regrets. Apologize; do not try to explain. Why belabor the end, sinking into the emotional slough of the blame game? Admit to the only truth worth saying: "We no longer understand one another." No moralizing. No rehashing. "We joyed, we suffered, we are." Mostly thank her for all the good parts of the relationship; embroider on a few of them if you have the grace. Emphasize how desirable she is. "I know what I am losing." Endings are as important as beginnings, and the Great Goddess gave you the gift of creativity and memory to make roses in December. Protect her self-respect and your own, and you may be on the way to the joys of *aprés-deux*.

Every wise old Lesbian also knows the above scenario is possible only when the attachment to a lover and to a relationship is loose, or when you have already worked your way through the grief of loss. What do you do when the break-up leaves you bleeding so badly you feel terminal, when your heart is shattered into a mosaic, when you are a walking vortex of pain? When you rise above suffering only to meet agony — the existential agony of impermanence, the mystery of evanescence? *Tout passe, tout casse, tout lasse.* You are so gutted you are sure you can never bear to tell your life story to anyone again. Here, then, are fifty, more or less, ways to cope with a serious break-up, fifty little tourniquets because as Yeats' Crazy Jane said to the Bishop, "Nothing can be sole or whole/That has not been rent."

Take solace that the following remedies were useful over the course of the twenty-two major break-ups collectively experienced within Lady Clitoressa's Circle. Each of us lived through times when she felt her heart was eroding like the Marin coast. And as Lady Clitoressa says, "Grief never leaves you where she finds you."

If you are in pain, you of course won't believe the truth that if you give away part of your heart, it will grow back. Just try to keep your heart open one more time, one more spring. As one of the greatest women poets of Japan, Izumi Shikibu, wrote a thousand years ago:

> Over the years
> I have grown used to sorrow.
> There is not one Spring
> I did not leave behind flowers.

The Descent into Darkness

It has been said that since we are all as Goddesses we may as well get good at it. One inescapable truth is that our pantheon holds the persona of the Dark Goddess. Though we never extend her an invitation, she is the guide who faithfully appears whenever our road to heaven forks due to a break-up. She promises (if you can hear her) that whenever you lose something, she will show you something (if you can see it). On this oblique note, she hurls you into the dark Void, the perilous *terra infirma* where creation is a matter of getting rid of something. The Dark Goddess could care less that she is unwelcome as the pilot of your fate. She sternly embodies *Lady Clitoressa's First Law of Dissolution: Libido does not exist without mortido.* Look at Persephone, Lilith, Oya, Inanna, Kali. The Dark Goddess wants you to understand the poet Audre Lorde's *I still salute/the power of learning/loss*, to take a tour of the psyche's "deeptown." Create your own poetry of loss wherever you can. Make sure it teaches you how to lick your own heart for moisture.

However you come to terms with the fact that you have now changed realms, the first step is to fully acknowledge the reality of loss and to let the pain flow. There may be shock and denial. You may bargain abjectly with your lover to return. You may carry around the corpse of the relationship, mooning over old photographs and letters. It is time to pull up your socks. You have gotten the message; now hang up the phone. This is often so hard to do that the Ladies suggest putting up signs around the house to help break the powerful denial spell. One made an applique of a Javanese proverb, "You can't get water from the moon." A favorite is the famous journal entry #298 from Ntozake Shange's *Sassafrass, Cypress & Indigo*. Like the beautiful Cypress, mourning her Lesbian love, we must learn to sing alone:

whatchu cant have you just cant have
who aint meant just aint in you
who be gone just aint there
what aint yrs/must be somebody else's
you gotta bring what you be needin
you gotta unwind-wound-down/take a look around
& bring what you be needin

List all your gifts, talents, generosities and achievements on slips of colored paper. Put them in a nice little jar on a sunny window sill. She may be gone, but the jar remains as full as ever. Face the hard truth that she does not want or recognize all your gifts. Leave the window open for her if you wish, but go back to the living, the doing, and let the dead bury the dead.

Once you are able to log in that the lover relationship is ended, over, you can look forward to utter depression. We in the divorce field say "look forward" because depression is the break-up stage in which you get to be somewhat numb. You are iced over with loneliness, otherwise vague and sad. Even if you are not normally a list-maker, this may be the time to write down what you need to do every day and pin it to your shirt, because nothing seems to matter. What is happening is that you are not quite able to process the pain yet, so the higher intelligence within is anesthetizing you as you fuel up for the emotional releases to come.

Above all, do not hole up in isolation for extended periods, or your other systems may shut down. Be quiet, but take long walks to keep the energy moving. Stay away from television, king of the downers. Instead, watch children playing, flowers growing and waves flowing. Ask friends to bring you hearty soups, then bless all the creature networks that make your food possible. Also ask friends to accompany you into the world for dinner and events, again so you don't contract into a self-fixated ball. Be sure to set up a circle of support because if there is just one friend on the case, she will burn out. Friends are the best vigilantes for rampant negative thinking, as your impaired thought processes now cast you as a failure, a social pariah.

While taking care not to isolate, recognize that one of the functions of good old down-time depression is to force you to spend hours with yourself, your own best friend, your ultimate healer. Every day perform a simple, caring act for yourself. Arrange yourself a bouquet, bake yourself cookies, bring yourself books from the library. Expensive art books are good; so are witty, even mordant, British novels. At first you may find it haunting to be alone. This is natural. The light often plays in interesting patterns and so does sound. A way to keep your sensibilities from ricocheting off the walls is to lightly channel them into writing, music, art. This may be an exceptionally gifted time. A work of art is often a wound that is healing. Just be sure to keep your feet warm and sleep a lot.

Do not be surprised when your glacier of depression splinters into panic. You realize that you cannot concentrate and fear that you are going off your rails. This is known as the Hour of the Wolf. Do not suppress it or it will haunt you again and again. Talk to someone to whom you can detail every fear. When your friends get weary of reassuring you that the whole world is not in a state of collapse and that you will not be carted off by the white shirts, you can pay a Lesbian therapist to help you. Get a shrink to fit! A most excellent book for Lesbians on finding a good therapist is *The Lavender Couch, A Consumer's Guide to Psychotherapy for Lesbians & Gay Men* by Dr. Marnie Hall. You can go free to meetings of Sex & Love Addicts Anonymous in many cities where there is an A.A. office to direct you to S.L.A. Misery not only loves company, but it benefits from shared experience, strength and hope. Another useful technique is to cry into the ever-sympathetic ear of your friends' answering machines. On your tape, save their return professions of faith in your sanity and recovery. In the wee hours, play them over and over with a purring cat in your lap.

You will, in time, calm down enough to appear normal to most observers. But almost as soon as you are able to focus, you'll be shooting out bolts of hostility. The prime target is, of course, your old lover. Anger often means that you are getting well, that you can feel again. Anger is useful when it helps to burn bridges and enable you to let go, especially if you have been ill-used. Write up all your grievances and ritually burn them to symbolize your new freedom from such barbarities. It is never wise, however, to commit your unfiltered outrage to a letter and send it. Angry "Dear Jane" letters rarely rise above churlish and self-righteous bleating. Letters are usually an unfair, unilateral form of punishment because you are still afraid to confront your old lover directly. Accept no suspected missile of recorded anger either. Reading her could set you back for months. Once I could not resist, "After agonizing for many minutes, I have decided to return your letter unopened," but it was a cheap shot. Be advised that any time you resort to the direct cut during a break-up, you show how much you are bleeding.

When you move into the stage of being angry with yourself — guilt — be especially careful. You can get fixated on what-I-did-wrong and drive yourself crazy again. It is all blood under the bridge now. You can only release guilt by exchanging it for responsibility. Guilt is a futile wallow in the past by the self-absorbed. Take responsibility for your sorry actions by making real amends where you can, and, above all, change how you behave in the present.

Forgive and be patient with yourself. Loss of a love is as painful as a physical body blow and usually takes longer to heal, sometimes a few months for the severe symptoms, sometimes more than a year until you feel totally like your old self again. Remember that besides psychic pain you are also going through what can only be called physical withdrawal. Not only are your arms literally empty, crying for what they miss, but your body is undergoing a chemical wallop. At the loss of a long-term partnership, many people's internally synthesized opiate-like hormone supplies drop off. Unfair, but true. If you are amazed at how tormenting your pain is, it may be that your usual chemical intermediaries have hit low ebb. Exercise is invaluable for alchemizing these relieving hormones into play again. Exercise and the outdoors also help to re-energize you because even in a bad relationship, the partner was a source of energy for you.

Sometimes the body will acknowledge grief before the mind does. The empty feeling in your solar plexus (the power chakra) reflects the loss of a certain identity. The voice can be immobilized, only tiny noises coming out at the back of the throat. The "sound of silence"? As you disengage and disidentify, disorientation is the natural follow-up. Here, periods, even short ones, of deep, slow breathing, counting from one to ten, can help. Luckily, the mind is like a turntable; it cannot play two selections at once. When your mind plays a mad squirrel cage song, do whatever works to lift its needle of attention. Meditate on something wordless like your breathing, the light and shadow on a tree, music notes rising and falling. Be forgiving of how often you slip back into squirrel cage rehash. Patiently lift the needle and gently place it on a soothing selection.

Despite this skill, you may find yourself beginning to doubt your whole identity, your identity as a Lesbian, your identity as a lover. Your daily life, future plans and priorities face reorientation. You may feel you have lost not only your lover, but also your best friend. All the cracks are opening up in life's floorboards. Thus Lady Clitoressa warns, "She who lacks time to mourn lacks time to mend." The grieving process takes courage and faith as well as time. A love relationship arouses dormant, primordial yearnings for things like unconditional love, dependency, permanence, truth. When our expectations of these seem crushed, we come face to face with the Void, with impermanence, with chaos. How do you keep your bearings now that the cup is neither half-full nor half-empty, just

141

half? How can the ordinary mind comprehend that the cup is now both empty and full, that, in fact, there is no container or contained? To deal with such irreducible questions takes much courage in the free association department. At least you are, well, free . . .

To make it all easier, we gay divorcees in Lady Clitoressa's Circle formed a group called "Friends of the Void." You send no money and get nothing in return. You are a full-fledged member as soon as your nest is empty, and you face the chaos of new beginnings. This chaos only looks fearful next to the old order. It is really a neutral zone of primal, fertile energy, unshaped by purpose, free to be anything. The Void is to be enjoyed. Buddhist thought holds that each moment is made up of sixty-five *ksanas* or instants (more or less), which are continually arising, disappearing, appearing. Thus, the Law of Impermanence is not a pessimistic understanding. Take the Friends motto, "Nothing is ever always." This will lead you to such profound meditations on the nature of impermanence that you may become religious in the sense of taking precious care of each moment arising. Your existence becomes as vast as your sense of the moment is vast. Stability is a story we make up.

Friends of the Void holds potlucks (we are, after all, Lesbians) to which one need bring nothing because no one is there. This does not impede the conversation from swirling around a favorite theme like "My Relationship as a Cosmic Set-Up," or "the Principle of Reverse Polarity," with readings by Yin and Yang of *I-Ching* fame. We always celebrate the great "Principle of Periodicity," toasting whatever cycle or season is unfolding. The best of times are when Absurdity regales us with her laughter, her laughter in the dark.

So, my sad friend, join us in Friends of the Void, where you are on your own, but not alone, where, considering the pain, the sweetest, saddest phrases in the Yoniverse are, "This too shall pass" and "Surely this is not without meaning."

Compost & Let Grow

There comes a time, only after some time, when you can begin to see *le luz de la lucha*, the light of the struggle. You have carefully felt where you hurt, you have asked yourself to benefit from the pain, and you have been able to come up with at least one thing in the world that gives you hope. You still may be "a harp in the wind," as George Sand put it, but you are on the road to recovery. For openers, you can be thankful or at least relieved about several things. The lack of emotional sobriety your relationship brought, with its disarray and crisis, is over. No longer do you have to worry, wonder and rehearse for the end of this three-legged race. List all of your old lover's irritating qualities which you never have to deal with again, not to mention outbreaks of her knavery, wretchedness, or downright perdition. Maybe her negatives are not that terrible, but chances are they neatly reinforce your own. Now you are released to practice elsewhere.

Where the Buddha is not,
Do not linger.
Where the Buddha is,
Put your finger.

When you have allowed room for the fools in you both, next make a list of all the good things you received from the relationship. The greater the feeling of loss, the more significant the gifts this woman probably brought you. The good ways your lover changed you are yours to keep. One Lesbian mother said she felt her old lover's presence even in her child because the lover's friendship had influenced her daughter so much. Loneliness fades. People become a part of one another on a level that remains. Each relationship is like a chrysalis. You leave it vulnerable, irredeemably altered, moving into the light.

One light to keep visualizing during this change of state is the possibility of friendship, the opening of the great *après-deux* relationship. Lovers are wonderful, but ex-lovers are forever. Here love does not die; it exists in a quieter place. Relationship scholars say that for a lover relationship to evolve into a deep friendship, there needs to be a healing time plus some resolution of whatever broke you up as lovers. You might use a mediator or couple counselor or talk issues through yourselves after time has mellowed things. Resolution is made difficult if another woman is involved because she often becomes the focus of the break-up, rather than the real conflicts which likely preceded her. Resolution may be impossible if self-destructive behavior is involved ('til drugs do us part), or if there are locked-in patterns like power games, battering, or neurotic dependency.

Some women need a long time of mourning alone before they can begin to work on friendship. Six months is not unusual. A period of separation from your old lover allows you to break old ties and begin to rebuild your life. You may risk a set back every time you see or talk to your old lover. Explosive reactions are the norm and rub salt in the wound. The sooner you get physical withdrawal over, the better; each exchange is another hook. You can make a date with your old lover, one, two, even six months down the line, for the express purpose of trying to resolve any remaining conflicts and to rebuild your relationship as friends. Why confuse endings with finality? Neither of you is dead. If she was worth loving once, she is worth loving now, and life is too short to be small. Why lose each other if you have a precious history and much in common? Remember the jewel of friendship when you are tempted to strike out at her or do something mean-minded in the throes of break-up. The less to clean up, the better. There is an art to losing something, to running your end of the ending. When you compost the layers of loss, something will grow out of them if you don't add the quicklime of spite.

Do not be surprised, however, if you and your old love continue to have some of the same difficulties. Remember that her chronic lateness, for example, or lack of tact will not have disappeared. The difference is that you are now free to focus on each other's positive qualities, reacting to the others with tolerance or irony, rather than hysteria. Above all, stay in the present. Levy a fine each time one of you starts sifting through the rubble of the past and mewling. You cannot be this immature and stay friends. If you must rehash old history, try to take the role of two generous, worldly reviewers, going over a book you once read. You will also have to work out new limits with each other, like time and sexuality boundaries. One of the nice things about *après-deux* is the likely undercurrent of sensuality, even if never acted upon. "You will always have a G-spot in my heart." After a "decent interval," you both may wish to ritualize your transformation from lover relationship to primary friendship. Such a ritual is described in the last chapter.

One vigorous private ritual to use to let go in the first place is called "Reconnecting the Chakras." Imagine this seven-horse chariot of energy along your spine. Put your feet on the ground and feel your roots going into the earth. Notice your red root chakra kindle from the fiery core of earth. Open your crown chakra to the heavens and feel the energy flow all around your chakras like a glowing figure eight. Slowly, lovingly clear and clean all seven chakras with lavender light. You probably feel tenderness and pain in the first three chakras and may see them as torn, tangled or bruised. Keep cleaning and knitting them with the lavender light. Now close the first chakra carefully and move on to clean and close the second and third. Clear the upper four chakras with light too, but leave them open with a lavender flame burning.

144

Now go back to the first chakra. See how many psychic golden cords of security have grown out to connect you with your former lover's first chakra? Disconnect these gently, but firmly, and reconnect them with your own heart chakra. Do the same in the second chakra of emotion, romance and sexuality, and then in the third chakra of ego expression and power. You may wish to disconnect the golden cords connecting your hearts, or you may not. You can leave connecting cords here because they are the energy of universal love and compassion without attachment. If you are leaving your heart connected to her, double check that all the old cords from your first three chakras are reconnected to your own heart. You may have no cords connecting you together in the upper three chakras because their energy is taken up with ethereal powers.

Be careful of yourself in doing this powerful ritual. Make sure you have someone whom you can call. Disconnecting any psychic cords is painful. You may feel like they leave round, deep burning scars. These will take time to heal. You may feel a great sense of loss and loneliness. Your energy level may be down for a while. You will be more careful now with whom you spin your golden cords. Your old lover may try to contact you. People can often feel when you have disconnected them.

You can use the compost of your old relationship to plant entirely new seeds of selfhood. In any traumatic situation, you have the choice of shutting down and protecting yourself or trying to learn and grow. If you immediately run into a new woman's arms, it is not likely that you will process and learn from the break-up. You will tend to repeat yourself again and again, using courtship as a diversion to cover up pain. Pain is a warning, a warning that you should pay attention to something significant. It is best to spend composting time loverless and to come face-to-face with yourself.

Have the courage to run what Lady Clitoressa calls a "relationship retrospective." Most people who have near-death experiences see a flashback of all the significant people in their lives. Why wait? What are your recurring relationship patterns? Your recurring roles? How do your relationships tend to begin, tend to end? What common qualities do all your partners share? Do you yourself possess any of the characteristics you fought in your old lover? Was she your shadow, brought in to connect you with your multi-sided energy patterns? What attracted you to her problems in the first place? What are your relationship strengths and weaknesses? What troubles have you caused others? Where did you arm and protect yourself? Where did you open up and grow? What do you want to learn to do differently? What do you want now? Do you want your lover to be happy more than you want her to be with you? What made you happy before you met her? Admit that it takes two people to drive a relationship into the ground. Even if your part in its death was only ten percent (ha!), face your responsibility for what it is. Make any amends that you can, and release everyone, including yourself. From it, you can begin to build a new, inner relationship. "Whenever we talk about relationships, we are really talking about ourselves in another form," says Lady Clitoressa.

Good Grief!

If you agree rationally and philosophically with most of the above, but you still feel like hell, here are a few more heart-mending exercises from the Ladies. Don't worry when waves of grief, doubt and anger rise and fall without warning. Your healing is likely to be a jagged line of "not-so-goods" and "betters," rather than a smooth curve of progress. Something which may help is a form of Zen-influenced teaching called "reality therapy" or "Morita" after its early Japanese founder. Its basic tenet is "behavior wags the tail of feelings." The Morita way is to note feelings and accept them: "To suppress a feeling is like smashing a wave with a hammer. This creates a thousand little waves." But the stoic advice of Morita is to go on and *do* whatever you need to regardless of mood. Your actions will ultimately then influence your emotions. Emotions may be considered the "spices" of existence, rather than the main course. Emotions need not determine our behavior or be "in tune" before we act. Here are further action-oriented suggestions that have worked for some of us in loss:

☆ To feel lovable again, do something loving for someone.

☆ To feel peace, meditate on peace and freedom from suffering for all beings, and do your part to create harmony, if it is only to speak gently.

☆ To feel positive, pursue quality thoughts when you can't summon up purely positive ones. For example, consider that although you may have met your old love in other lives or have karmic connections, it is impossible for you ever to lose your "soul-mate." Soul-mates are for life, so they never incarnate at the same time in the earth realm. They are always at your side to support and guide you. We can't have a soul-mate nodding out on Valium or falling through the ice. Another thought: reconsider the myth that being loved by a partner and happiness are somehow fused. Many people so love the world or a true or beautiful part of it that they live

146

in uncoupled love and delight. In contrast, many people who are loved are the angels of misery — as are their partners. For other quality thoughts, read or listen to a favorite teacher you have been neglecting.

☆ There are intelligent and caring books about breaking up. *Rebuilding* by Bruce Fisher is one of the best, even if it is het. *Unbroken Ties: Lesbian Ex-Lovers* by Carol Becker is an anatomy of the Lesbian break-up, and it is unintentionally funny in accurately portraying our intense overacting during the throes. Chapter Five, in the *Sex & Love Addicts Anonymous Handbook*, "Withdrawal," is strong tonic when you can handle it.

☆ Ritualize your life during these turbulent times into routines as beautiful and simple as you can make them. This is especially important if you freelance or don't have a work-a-day job to give you structure. Doing simple meditative tasks makes you feel worthy without overwhelming you. I stripped my redwood doors during one dark winter of my heart. Their wild, laughing grain cheers me to this day.

☆ Light candles, burn incense and tune into any rose quartz and red coral you can beg, borrow or buy.

☆ Get whatever professional reinforcements you need to help your amuse system kick in. The world is full of humorists awaiting you: witty authors in the library, comedy movies and videos, local comedians. Some of the greatest black — and silver — humor is found in twelve-step meetings. Laughter is the gentle jogging which gets your heart back into shape.

☆ Pretend you are visiting a very sick friend and trying to cheer her up in this life. The conversation turns to "How My Relationship Died." Your job is to make this poor woman laugh, not to play the Devil's Martyr. Roll out the most absurd highlights, ridiculous arguments and bizarre behavior of your break-up. You will start laughing yourself. We may be by nature a tragedy, but by action we are a comedy.

☆ This exercise is for veteran hippies with a Ph.D. in LSD. For 35,000 years cultures have used altered states of consciousness in healing. Either the sufferer altered her consciousness with a sacred drug or went to a healer or shaman with non-ordinary consciousness. When your fixated, filtered reality is almost too hard to bear, why not relax your brain channels to find the past is not what you thought, nor is the present?

Jump into the quantum soup. Open up your cosmic detachment to attachment and rekindle your genuine fascination for life's quirks. Note that your heart will feel the incision of a snowflake or two, but you can usually discover, as Alice Munro describes, a "queer kind of pleasure" in seeing how the design didn't fit and the center couldn't hold. If to achieve connection is to court chaos and contradiction, why not travel in the exquisite laughter of swirl and swim?

☆ Now a message from the Narcotics Division. Scrupulously avoid alcohol and ordinary dope. We want you to tune in, not out. Most mood-altering drugs short-circuit your feelings to actually prevent you from coming to terms with pain, intimacy, even pleasure. You get a chemical lobotomy, not a healing. Chemical coping drowns out exactly who you need — your soul-mate — and can leave your entire life on the rocks. It is said that the woman who would order her life may have to send back the wine.

☆ Do a "geographic cure" if at all possible. A powerful way to break the spell of misery is to totally remove yourself from the scene of angst for a while. Your old lover's favorite chair, her gifts, "our" songs on all the tapes elicit migraines of pain. Staying with a friend or house-sitting for even a weekend will help you to snap out of hypnotic doldrums.

☆ Beg, borrow or buy new tapes so that you can use music to heal yourself. The combination of booze, "our" old songs or country and western music is a one-way ticket to purgatory.

☆ Speaking of purgatory, a most gruesome one is when you have broken up, but still have to live together until one of you finds a new place. This is a test of every psychic strength you possess, every claim to good manners and sweet forbearance. First of all, spend as little time at home as possible. No one can sustain equanimity in this situation. Pretend that you are a great actor in your greatest role, "Attractive Stranger." Think "spaciousness." Or pretend you are a wise and compassionate priest of the Goddess who has been sent into the Valley of Pain and Indignity to learn softness and grace. They say it is not necessary to be a Buddha, only to act like one. If you are living in the eye of such torment, take solace in the fact that having had such purgatory on earth, you will escape all punishment in the hereafter.

☆ If you are lucky enough to escape "Rooming with my Ex," another rough play is called "Long Division," or who gets the sheltie and who gets the shaft. If you lived together, the time comes for custody decisions over the Cuisinart, the aquarium, or, Goddess help us, the futon, and even the friends. Ideally, most of this was decided long ago in your "Accords." If not, it's rough seas ahead. Material goods often come to symbolize emotional injustices to be righted. In most of the Ladies' memories of the "Best Break-Up," each partner went far out of her way to be generous. "This is my gift to you." These couples usually remain heart-friends with lots of shared resources to this day. You will probably hate whatever you have to wrestle from your old lover, so why not let a few things go gracefully and keep your dignity?

Kids are something else. Ideally, again, you worked out your visitation rights, support, and other issues, when things were calm. It is always best to tell children the truth about events and about your real feelings. Children can summon up a lot of healing wisdom to take care of themselves. But be prepared to talk about their issues, which are not far different from your own: issues of abandonment, dependence, stability, blame.

Also be prepared to deal with other biological family. It is likely that parents and siblings who supported you in your Lesbian relationship will support you in a break-up. Families who were hostile to your relationship will likely remain judgmental and blaming in a break-up. Perhaps the saddest thing, however, is that if our Lesbianism is invisible to our first family, so is the pain of our break-ups.

☆ Many women find that "logging" their grief in a notebook is very self-supporting. Keep track of the emotional binges, and what tends to bring them on. Write out what sustains you, what you cherish. Reinvent yourself as a character who is coming home.

☆ Write up your present obituary. Write out what you would like it to say five years from now.

☆ Put up affirmative signs like, "So You Blew It. Start Over." "I Have the Rest of My Life Back." "Pain Is Unavoidable. Suffering Is Optional."

☆ Develop parts of yourself you never had time for before. Art, politics, community service are also great ways to invite new people into your life.

☆ Wholeheartedly invite new people into your life. Nature abhors a vacuum. While you are free to grow alone, you are also free to find the one looking for you.

☆ Be sure to set it up at first so that you are spending holidays with other people. Holidays are famous loneliness spirals. Also ask friends to be with you at times that are especially bleak, like anniversaries.

☆ When the robe is change, wear it. Change brought her and change took her. Some women like to get new clothes, a new hair style, a new job — they change everything but the kids.

Thus endeth this unpopular chapter. But if we are all lovers who walk alone — sometimes — is it *the* end? It sounds more like the beginning of something new, because that is what endings are for. "Go easy," Gertrude Stein directs, "and if you can't go easy, go as easy as you can."

VIII.
Ceremonies of
Lesbian Life:

Rites & Rituals

T he simple reason that Lesbians are great ritualists is that Lesbians are great lovers. Every truly great ritual is fired in love's wonder, faith and reverence: love of the earth, love of the Source in all Her Mystery, love of celebration, love of creativity's change and cycle, love of self and others. If not "spiritual," all Lesbians could at least be called "high-spirited," to be able to love in a world that hates and persecutes us for that very feeling. But our ancient mothers, after all, invented religion. Priesthood is women's oldest profession. The brilliant Sappho was the High Priestess of none other than Aphrodite, the Goddess of Love. Sappho was more than a Socrates to her school on Lesbos because she was a sublime poet with a philosophy broad enough to enfold religion itself.

Yes, our women's sacred voices have been stifled these last few thousand years by violent, pathogenic weapons created by a thinking unnatural to us. Yes, our songs have been muted behind the walls built to separate us, to contain our awesome sensuality, to silence our laughter. Yes, our traditions have been twisted by lies, our psychic powers denied, our divinity blasphemed. And YES, most heartily, the Goddess of Ten Thousand Names has now lost her patience. Our womanpower, our womanspirit is awakening to shake and transform ourselves and society. The ancient voice of women's wisdom, 35,000 years of matrifocal earth wisdom, is again the incoming tide. Women kiss each other in ecstasy — in the streets — as we did in the Priestess Sappho's time and long before. Mother, Daughter and Holy Lover, we touch each other again, deeply enough to summon all women past, present, and future. Each woman kisses another awake, in a sunrise that cannot be dimmed.

One of our most light-giving powers is the evolution of Lesbian sacred ritual: our own rites of interconnectedness, of re-membering, of empowerment, of harmony, of the Great Moon and the Seasonal Wheel. These rituals open us to the merging of lightness and dark, to death and rebirth, to star and space. At first, I rolled my eyes when the Ladies radiated what I saw as Hail Mary moonshine and Pagan glade grandiloquence. Then, I got the message. We were talking power here. Seventeenth century Salem roared into Los Angeles. After years of seeing witch hunts of communists, queers, humanists and liberals, the boys were again on the trail of the real item. One of us, Z. Budapest, was arrested in 1975 for celebrating women's divination, Witchcraft. Surprise! Witches began coming out of the broom closet with bells on. With her many high spirits, Z. flew off to fame and good fortune.

Things began to look up, but our very cells' anguished memories are also stirring within us. We feel the *Old Testament* time when women-honoring cultures were shattered by absolutists of a tyrant god, Yahweh, to whom women are an abomination. We smell the Burning Time when nine million women were executed for being healers, teachers, artists, Lesbians, free thinkers, or just plain different or frail. In some towns, all women were exterminated by fire. We live during the Surgical Time when women are drugged, electro-shocked or cut. Our cells carry ancient/present fear and pain, but these now opened wounds can be cleansed.

All our lives, we've seen a paranoid status quo ceaselessly harass change agents. Today's Lesbian Witches (from the Celtic *wicca*, to bend, shape, change) indeed believe in the old nature wisdom — also called the "new physics" — that in our whirl-of-energy world change is natural, inevitable. Change herself, in dancing disguise, is our constant. Another great Wicca essence is her profound reverence for the three-fold natural forces of birth, nurturance and clearing away, the Triple Goddess of creativity, love and death. Since *"thea"* means Goddess, the theology of Wicca is the*a*logy. The Triple Goddess is far beyond any limiting, static definition, so Her liturgy is evocative metaphor, her mass is poetry.

Witches also hold that individual freedom plus her sister, responsibility, are sacred to being. "Do As Thou Wilt, and Harm None" is the creed of the free Lesbian too. Best of all, Witches celebrate that we are really born — and borne — in wonder, not in suffering and guilt, not in fear and craving. The boys who are running the big protection racket of the last few thousand years emphasize these dreadfuls to scare us. They lied about everything else, and they had reason to lie about the "danger" of Witchcraft. Her danger is only to masculinist values. Wicca has no concept of devil worship; satanism is a Christian heresy. Let's face it; if you consider yourself a Lesbian eco-feminist, you are probably a Witch. Lady Clitoressa says that if we must have labels, let us be promiscuous with them. Do not be afraid that you can change the world.

Meantime, so-called "New Age" Lesbian feminists are rediscovering what is actually Old-Time Religion, the religion of the Creatrix-Goddess honored for at least 35,000 years by native peoples. They are also tapping into the healing teachings of Taoism,

154

Buddhism and Yoga, the lush earth wisdom of Native American and Afro-Caribbean traditions. In these worldviews, female energy is given the place of honor for its receptive, vibrant womb-darkness and its deeply sensual, diffuse awareness, an awareness leading us to a sense of interconnectedness and belonging. The cults of Jesus, Buddha and Jewish wisdom are also being re-visioned by Lesbians to uncover their older, intrinsic life-force teachings, later polluted by writers with masculinist anger and fear. Further, these women are demanding full ordination. It is no accident that a majority of practicing ritualists and spokeswomen in women's spirituality movements are Lesbians or are the many-aspected women whc stand with their Lesbian sisters to champion the pleasure, creation and divinity of all forms of love.

Nor is it any accident that most Lesbians who remain in movements for social change practice some form of spiritual ritual such as meditation, moving meditation, or ceremony. Lesbian music "shamans" galvanized our early movement with healing ceremonies of song and unity. Spirituality and song are intimate partners in every ongoing political movement. The intuitive, right-brain "irrational" activities of ritual open our deep transformative consciousness, called variously Higher Presence, Spirit Guide, Source, Changing Woman. This Flow/Being provides currents of encouragement, wisdom, compassion and protection, even "altered" states. Right brain taps into analogical and "ego-logical" thinking. Ritual activities also open us up to timeless here-and-now being, wherein each moment of honorable struggle is most certainly a moment of victory. Whenever you can conceive of past/present/future as a seamless, evolutionary continuum, you can relax, knowing you have as many lives as you need to finish your work. You have been here many times before in your physical and spiritual ancestors. You will be here again and again in all the hearts you touch.

Notice Lesbians who regularly take risks — and most of us do every day in sheer loyalty to our lifestyle — have a much easier time of it if they have a spiritual practice. Let's take an extreme example: Lesbians who risk jail, offering their own bodies for civil rights or peace. No strip search can confiscate the sword of a spiritual practice. If arrested with a group, ritual theater and dance make marvelous entertainment in the barren landscape. Quiet, contemplative meditation is grounding, revelatory and relaxing; moving meditation provides fine exercise. Practice in ritual fasting is helpful since no food is often better than the sinisterly processed jail fare of carbs, caffeine and catsup. A spiritual practice is common sense in any jolting situation similar to jail, where you have only one option:

"You can do your time easy or you can do your time hard." A simple spiritual ritual is a place to stop and figure out how to "breathe easy." The Ladies say, "It is a place where, when all else is gone, you can dance in your soul."

Ritual as a Door of Perception

Why do Lesbians create ritual? Because society at large has tried to rob us of our Lesbian traditions, our spiritual path of love, our soul's identity. Judy Grahn's *Another Mother Tongue: Gay Words, Gay Worlds*, the breath-taking chronicle of historic Lesbian and gay cultural symbols, traditions, celebrations and magic, reveals the mother lode of our ancient glittering roots in the darkness. Still, like a despised ethnic group, we are basically denied our roots and customs — and with them a source of deep strength. Our committed unions, unlike heterosexual marriages, are given no respect, much less affirmation and protection. Many of us have been banished or alienated from our biological families' seasonal celebrations and denied church rituals of love and community. When our loved ones separate from us or die, there are none of the usual social rites for support and healing; even newspaper obituaries usually expunge the very name of the most loving survivor. The enormousness of our coming-out initiation ritual draws a total blank or is viciously misunderstood. Inescapable Valentine's Day is relentlessly hetero-*sexual*, while our erotic, spiritual celebrations at times like Gay Pride Day, *Mardi Gras*, May Day and Halloween are considered "too blatant." (They are certainly more frequent, which says something.) And where is Single Mother's Day? She deserves a week. Lesbians are ceasing to act like beggars at the rich, hollow feast days run by the pale brotherhood for the pale brotherhood. Each Lesbian is realizing that she can be a priestess of her own vital ceremonies of creativity, letting go and renaissance. We can enact the beauty of the ancient rituals while weaving in our own.

All of us have profound and recurrent spiritual needs. We need to "be present" with the "whys," the invincible mysteries of life's dance. Why does the universe pulse in cycles like the love act? What kind of consort am I to Her? What aspect shall We play today? We also have an abiding need to express our reverence and awe with the "hows" of the universe, the delicate intensity that can split a seed to grow, the power that can explode a sun into gold. "As in Heaven, so on Earth." The deepest whys and hows of our daily activities are questions of equal significance. Masculinist technological answers are of little help. High technology reflects values of control, not those of *respect*. Technological, scientific information can never replace respect in dealing with an intricate, miraculous ecological tapestry whose infinitely complex weave is forever changing. Even as giant telescopes and electronic microscopes reveal ever more threads, deeper connections and harmony, men try harder to "master" it all, wrenching things around for the short fall. Because this is an act of will and not of vision, every creature is now saddled with the wretched dissonance and havoc of a nearly toxic planet.

We are crying for a vision. Rites and rituals are avenues of vision, ways to enact stockpiles of unexpressed feeling, awe and possibility. Rituals are focused times when we can affirm our capacity for personal and planetary regeneration, for community revitalization. Here we can feel the living, non-static process of being, one moving toward the fulfillment of a vision. As the womanspirit performance artist/scholar Hallie Iglehart Austen says, "We are all creation makers, and a new world is awaiting creation."

Lady Clitoressa once said, "Our lives are rituals of coming and going." I think of her many personal, private ones. Each dawn, Lady Clitoressa lights incense to her benign, flowing statue of Kwan-Yin, the Chinese Goddess of Compassion. A Goddess welcoming one with a little bouquet of fresh flowers or a sprig of green is a far from grumpy way to begin the day. Every chill coastal morning Lady Clitoressa lovingly makes a fire. Alone in the half-light, she reverently eats her fruit and hot cereal before it. This is her Poetry Time. She waits, open, every day. Veils of fragrance rise from her tea. The fire gives itself in a passion that is more than enough. The Lady writes down some of what she receives in poetry to share with others.

Another of the Ladies finds poetry-time simply in standing before her window in the first morning light and winding her grandmother's round, golden pocket watch, engraved with her Grandmother's name, "Faith." Someone else does a Yoga "Salute to the Sun." She says she is most happy doing this at sunset, physically stretching back to her childhood on Key West, where everyone pauses and gathers in a public place to applaud the sun as it goes down. Moon ritual is greatly beloved by the Ladies, and we often meet in "moontime."

One of the Ladies does a "power ritual" every full moon. She leaves a crimson bowl of pure spring water outside all night, under the moon. It absorbs moonbeams. She anoints everyone in the household with drops of "moonbeam mix," even the cats who purr loudly.

The moon manifests the Great Goddess of Change. She takes her eloquent place in the heavens to endlessly, patiently reveal that all of life is a sacred rhythmic cycle, all eternity is a spiral hoop. The moon reassures us that not only are rising fullness and emptying the natural flow of being, but that this cycle is unending. She shows us that "be-ing" is a verb. The moon walks three nights in darkness, in the realm of death, but she has never broken her promise to return to the light. Her inimitable phases are the rhythm of the entire wheel of the year: beginning, waxing, harvest, death and beginning again. For all creatures' lifetimes, for molecule and mountain, it is the same rhythm.

The Goddess' own moonblood flows in each woman's womb where we too can begin life, fruit and let it go, only to begin again each lunation. Lunar cycles affect all the body's biorhythms, especially in natural surroundings, where man-made interference does not disturb the moon's powerful light energy and electromagnetic force. Most of our holidays (holy days) had lunar origins. The rituals of the Ladies are always moon-conscious, acknowledging essential powers of her particular phase.

Life has more luminosity when we stop to focus on our daily rituals. Often we perform our daily rituals on automatic pilot, rather than acknowledging how precious many of them are: caring for our bodies; making our living space clean and beautiful; greeting loved ones as aspects of the Goddess; beginning, practicing, and ending projects as though we are actually donating our life to them. The more focus on personal ritual, the more joy and appreciation it brings. Being awake, you can also see when a regular ritual does not help, but hinders. Never underestimate the power of any ritual to imprint a message and shape behavior. Personal rituals that do not work might be called bad habits or addictions. Many studies on alcohol ("spirits") addiction show that the addictive personality may often be the personality of greatest spiritual yearning and gifts, the one most crying for a vision. The wine is but a finger pointing at the moon, one wavering mightily.

Ritual as Theater

I asked each Lady in The Circle to remember a ritual that worked for her as a Lesbian, and what need it answered. For Constance, a great appeal of ritual is its beauty as art — participatory art performances with women. It invigorated her imagination and spirit to be with a group of Lesbian moms who, during the Spring Equinox, informally acted out the Great Mother/Daughter Death/

Rebirth saga of Earth Mother Demeter's love for her daughter Persephone. When Earth's daughter must live part of the year in the Underworld, it is the winter season in Earth's heart; her return marks the flowering and fruiting of the land. "I do not need to tell you the modern equivalents of Hades we enacted, like legal persecution and welfare hell." Myth provides the "screenplay" of many rituals, and women are hungry to play our stories, our heroes. "Poetry, song, dance, costumes and sets weren't elaborate; most things were filled in by the imagination. The main theatrical touch was to paint the faces of the women who played Persephone, Demeter and Hecate. The faces of Hades were covered by black nylons."

Because the action was immediate and participatory, Constance felt an involvement she never could at a twenty-million-dollar movie or in an $85 box seat at the opera. Informal rituals become manifest as they are enacted in a grand style, as articulate and visible as they were in the games of our childhood. "Some call it ritual. I call it adult play." Constance is not a mother, but a godmother, a "faerie godmother" to two children. "I enjoyed the play and the theater, but I got to thinking too, 'What is *my* myth with my godchildren? Will I be as alert and wise as the Night Rider Hecate to hear their cries and think of a way to trick Hades? What about the rest of my life; what myth am I living?' "

Ritual as Celebration

Harmony loves ritual because she loves to laugh and celebrate. As a recovering Jehovah's Witness, she needs to strengthen her amuse system. She took Lady Clitoressa's dictum to heart: "Joy is the most infallible sign of the Goddess." The Goddess' "Wheel of the Year," with four solstice/equinox days and the four cross-quarter celebrations, Candlemas, May Day, Lammas and Halloween, provide eight great feasts and lightings of fires when Harmony can gather with her sisters to affirm life's joyful, cyclic goodness. These days focus on the Creatrix, not the crucified, so there is dancing and singing. The rituals are times of toasting gratitude to earth's bounty and her light ever returning.

Harmony's favorite day is May Day, and she leaves May Baskets for her friends and a secret one for an old woman who speaks to no one. She and her lover decorate a May Pole, their shish kebab eucalyptus, with faerie lights and ornaments, and they have a party to dance around it. Her lover calls it "The Liberty Tree," because that is what this "tree of life" became in the French Revolution. Her lover persuades everyone to also celebrate May Day as International

Workers' Day because the old European and Russian socialists began this as a tradition. The U.S. Government freaked out in response and named this ancient day of frolic and freedom "Law Day." The Goddess winks.

Ritual as Rebirth

Lady Clitoressa is a child of the wintersong, "presented with the gift of life at the end of the day, at the end of the week, at the end of the month, at the end of a year, at the end of a century." For almost fifty years, she has celebrated the "Awakening of the Light," a Winter Solstice fire ritual that has become so well known that Lesbians have taken it to Europe and Australia. It all began when she had lost — well, everything. Her great love of thirteen years had died of cancer. Youth had passed into mid-life. A tentative new relationship with a much younger woman was over. Books accepted for publication were killed due to the paper shortages of World War II. Lady Clitoressa was realizing that her new, hard-fought career in freelance journalism would always be "life on the edge." So, she did exactly what many women do "with no prospects." She made herself a home. In 1940, for her last $700, "I bought a huddle of wood that no one else could consider a house. It was on a steep bit of hillside at the end of a road with a few other ghost houses, once summer cabins, abandoned, rotting. The beautiful land promised healing."

Regeneration and hope the land provided — beginning with a ritual. All alone during the Yule season, Lady Clitoressa decided she would try to begin repairs on the little "huddle." She was caught there at night in torrential rains, which began lashing the cabin's frail moorings like a ship. Terrified by the storm, terrified by life's bleakness, Lady Clitoressa wondered if the fireplace would draw to provide any light and warmth. The fire not only started; it roared a triumphal retort to the storm.

She thought she was alone. "Yet, as I added twigs and dry boughs, then madrone logs, the firelit room became peopled by presences: spirits of women. Women I had known: mother, grandmother, elder aunts, and back, back, all the women through the ages who kindled and tended sacred and domestic fires . . .

"My thought revolved around the recent transitions of my life: from city to country, concrete to earth, from rented flat to my own space, from the death of a beloved and a tumultuous relationship to solitude. As the rain poured down and the storm shook the small redwood house, there was born the possibility of a joyous sense of *connectedness*. A tilting storm-battered house, an emotionally and

economically precarious era, at the doorstep of midlife with no
obvious achievement other than survival: none of them mattered.
Deeply inward, something new was happening.

"I watched the burning madrone logs contribute to one another's glow, each keeping the other alight. I again felt the presence of
the women who had been familiars of this element. I heard their
voices telling me: 'This fire on your hearth is neither individual nor
separate any more than your living self is separate from us. We are
part of one another as your small blaze is part of our chains of fires
linking the centuries, a spark of the cosmic element itself . . . '

"In the morning, the first dawn of my renewed life, the still
smoldering cores of the logs seemed to be telling me what to do.
Madrone wood burns like coal. I placed it on a small metal dustpan
and took the logs out into the gently rainy morning, there to
become charcoal as they quickly ceased consuming themselves.
When the remains of my Solstice Fire had cooled, I wrapped them in
foil tied with a piece of red ribbon and placed them on the shelf
above the growing woodpile. This became the first of all the sub-
sequent Solstice Fire Logs, each to kindle the next, for all the years of
my life up to the present. When I finally moved to the place I call
Druid Heights, the most precious of all I took with me was the residue of the last fire in Madrona. My poem, 'Chains of Fires,' was
slowly shaped from this ritual, dictated by the women who visited
me that mid-winter dusk."

Chains of Fires

Each dawn, kneeling before my hearth,
Placing stick, crossing stick
On dry eucalyptus bark,
Now the larger boughs, the log
(With thanks to the tree for its life)
Touching the match, waiting for creeping flame,
I know myself linked by chains of fires
To every woman who has kept a hearth.

In the resinous smoke
I smell hut and castle and cave,
Mansion and hovel,
See in the shifting flame my mother
And grandmothers out over the world
Time through, back to the paleolithic
In rock shelters where flint first struck sparks

(Sparks aeons later alive on my hearth).
I see mothers, grandmothers back to beginnings,
Huddled beside holes in the earth
Of iglu, tipi, cabin,
Guarding the magic no other being has learned.
Awed, reverent, before the sacred fire
Sharing live coals with the tribe.

For no one owns or can own fire.
It lends itself.
Every hearth-keeper has known this.
Hearth-less, lighting one candle in the dark
We know it today.
Fire lends itself.
Serving our life.
Serving fire,
At Winter Solstice, kindling new fire
With sparks of the old
From black coals of the old,
Seeing them glow again,
Shuddering with the mystery,
We know the terror of rebirth.

Lady Clitoressa's ritual of re-membering, touching souls with our foremothers, and lighting our future, is now celebrated by the Circle. We first bless the "seed" of the charcoal, the wood nourished by earth, air and water, its blackness storing the birth of the sun. The room is dark, the longest night of the year. As the flames rise, each woman, one by one, approaches the fire, "trances" into it, and offers a small pine bough. The needles flare as each woman silently names something from the year she wants or needs to let go of. She bows, and pauses to say good-bye. Then she lights a new candle from the fire. At the end of the ritual, the room is a festival of lights. We all lift our candles in a joyous shout to the "Awakening of the Light." Each woman takes her candle home to light her next year's Solstice Fire and other "chains of fires" with loved ones.

Ritual as Community Building

With the birth of the sun and its climb higher into the sky, Lady Clitoressa needs help with her huge garden. So began the ritual of "Earth Mother's Day" one Mother's Day, but any sunny day is a fine time. Such a celebration and working together brought up a wonderful aspect of ritual (besides sheer earthiness), which is ritual's ability to foster community. Our picnic, with libations to the land and to each other, and the gardening together create a bond between people, many of whom are strangers, and a bond with the land, its resources and other species.

Of course, there is nothing like group energy focused on an individual in need to transform things; this is how healing works in a group ritual of "laying on of hands." Before we begin an Earth Mother's Day, we all stand in a circle with our hands on each other's necks in a symbol of trust and unity. We invoke the Goddess to "Let Light & Love & Power/Restore the Plan of Earth." We sing as we work. That first Earth Mother's Day, I looked up from a tall artichoke frond to find myself looking right down a beautiful woman's shirt. With all flustered and due respect, I spoke to her ardently of artichokes. The green artichoke hearts laughed all around us, and thus began a ritual within a ritual. This is why the Ladies say, "Ceremonies represent the ways of Heaven."

Ritual as Invocation

It is the "Queen of Heaven" aspect that Zenia loves in ritual, the "Manifest Deity" of it all. She wants to recreate the miraculous metaphor of the Goddess: The Cosmic Round, The Awakened One, the One in All/All in One. As the candles appear at Her ritual, each candle contributes to the total light aura, while each candle is a separate vehicle of light. "So in ritual, can we experience our own being as the Light of many/One. We feel our own power to bathe and to be bathed by the Source."

To Zenia, the symbols of the Goddess catalyze electrifying power. "I *know*, past mere belief, the Goddess is a fount of energy, that we women of the species most easily access and manifest this sacred energy. Creation itself, like all beings, birthed from the Womb. If there was a 'big bang,' it must have been a laugh when the Mother came in chaos, in an orgasm of organization. Woman was always, until the last five-thousand-year detour, the Creation Maker. The first human prototype is female; only secondarily may a fetus become altered with male characteristics. This is part of woman's capacity for androgyny, to be able to produce both female and male. Woman is the one not only to miraculously produce children from her own blood, but to alchemize this blood into milk. Woman's moon/season cycles are those of the Universe.

"We are each myriad, unique channels of Her charisma: creating, nourishing, clearing away. It is in ritual we focus on becoming transformer, conductor and mobilizer of this divine energy. The

163

group rite called 'raising the cone of power,' as well as ritual trance and ecstasy, give us contact with 'extraordinary' consciousness. Here we can align ourselves with the essential energy of creation, the changing, transformative cycles of life. Ritual worship of the Triple Goddess makes it possible to join the Plains of Heaven, the Earth, and the Depths. The meaning is whole, yet shining on many levels."

Zenia's beloved ritual is the Witches' New Year, All Hallows, or the Feast of the Ancestors. "At this time the veil between the realms of life and death is thinnest, psychic and divinatory powers strongest. Starlight and moonlight grow more powerful as the nights lengthen. The All Hallows' ritual belongs to Hecate, Queen of the Night. We accept Her cycle of darkness, from warm, quiet nesting to its wild forms of chaos, destruction and death. We learn to honor the Destroyer. She, too, has Her place. Hecate cries, 'Do not cling — or the cycle will waver, harmony be destroyed, orbits fall!' We explore grief, going deep, letting go, turning inward to face our darkest shadow, our deepest vulnerability.

"Hecate, Queen of the Crossroads, brings her sisters wisdom, the powers of going on; She gives us protection and vengeance. We remember the Burning Times and vow strength. The blood of the pomegranate, our rubyfruit, flows as we taste the red, tart seeds of life. The destiny of each seed is to die — to die into a seedling or to form nourishment for something. We set out food and flowers for the ancestors, who walk this night. They share their stories through our telling of them. We dance the Spiral Dance with them and feast until morning. Even the Queen of Night will not hold back the dawn."

Ritual as Healing

For Scarlett, the live-on-the-edge Lady, the lover who walks alone, a great act of ritual is its healing song. As soft bodies in a hard world, we all get bruised. Scarlett uses ritual to bounce back. For example, when she lost a job for being gay, the Ladies did such a job of exorcising the mean-mindedness, she felt lucky to be gone. "We did a call-and-response to gay hate/fear epithets with Lesbian Love 'Whoopee.' We answer 'Lesbians are deeepraved' with 'Lesbians are deelighted,' and so on. The 'Whoopee' always drowns out the fear, and we all hug and hug.

"Best of all, there was affirmation of me and hope for finding good work. Each woman brought a little soil from her favorite place. Someone brought shining, coarse white sand like they use in sacred sand and stone gardens. There was 'plum blossom' soil from under a flowering plum, homemade black compost and rich smelling cocoa-hulls. As each woman sifted her offering into a flat bowl, she told me how some competency of mine had helped or impressed her. 'This is your Earth Resume.' We planted quick-sprouting radish and alfalfa seeds in the bowl's mix. When they popped up, I felt such hope. I was told to eat them in salads; the radish sprouts are quite zesty. I don't know if their energy transmuted my luck, or their growing gave me courage, but I got through some hard times. By the time I'd sprouted every kind of salad sprout there is (fenugreeks are the most lusty), I got a great job with, of all people, a Lesbian real estate broker."

Here is another ritual someone told which provides a visible sign of hope amid bleakness, healing amid the broken. Break three earth-brown eggs with great flourish. Save the shells for garden mulch and rinse out two of the larger halves. Mix the eggs in wild delight with a couple spoonfuls of water. Sizzle them in a pan with grated cheese, chives and red bell pepper. Serve it forth. Tell your sad lover (who may be yourself), "If you don't break an egg, you can't have an omelet." Feed it to her with kisses (or kiss yourself three times on the soft inside of the elbow). Drink sparkling cider or champagne from the largest egg cups.

A very important rite is to support and guide each other through "the dark night of the soul," even beyond stark terror. An incest or rape healing ritual often involves moving through a "re-birth canal" to a regenerated, more powerful self. One version of this is to travel under a tunnel of women's legs, then rise to pass under the arch of their raised arms. Finally, trust five women to lift you to Heaven's healing protection.

A Basic Recipe for Ritual

This is akin to presenting you with a basic recipe for dinner — impossible, but fun to try. Ritual art has a few universals with infinite variations, just like any great pastime. And you, of course, have the always creative Lesbian edge. Remember when you learned to cook? For dinner, a consummate ritual if there ever was one, you gather some pots and pans and accumulate a few key herbs and spices. You select a menu, mind the oven, and taste everything with gusto. For a ritual, your vessel focus is the altar. Your herbs (plants) literally flavor the ritual if you eat them, and they produce the sweet fragrance, beauty and "green spirituality" of a key ritual ingredient, Earth. The spice of a ritual, carrying beyond it the mundane, is anything that invigorates or harmonizes your senses: candles, incense, scented oils, crystals, rainbow prisms, feathered plumes, and, of course, poetry, music, movement, even kisses. The omnipresent salt is the sacred spice of purification; salt preserves food from decay and salt water cleanses wounds. In ritual, "the stove to mind" is the cauldron of energy transformation. A dramatic symbol of this psychic transformation is the sacred Fire we light, transmuting matter into heat and light. The "menu" of a ritual is its main focus, overall plan or purpose: to give thanks, heal, gather power, create union, open up super-censory realms — perhaps all of these.

The great "gusto" of Lesbian ritual is the creative force of our imaginations. There are universals, even a loose structure, such as the sacred circle pattern, calling in the Four Elements, sharing food, but the liturgy of our ritual changes with the seasons and the season of our heart. We let improvisation and intuition roll. This is, after all, sacred play. Our rituals are protean, not procrustean. This is why a Lesbian at a tightly controlled, hierarchical ceremony may feel like a cat on a leash.

We may use a High Priestess or "Mother of the Spirit" as a theater director, and certain women may "act" as Goddess vehicles. Our ritual is a story whose rhythm is the beauty of every woman. The ritual has infinite numbers of whirling aspects, not hierarchical layers. Lesbians are not content to break the rules; we are remaking them. We hear the French writer and visionary Monique Wittig, in *Les Guérillères*: "There was a time when you were not a slave, remember that. You walked alone, full of laughter. You bathed barebellied. You say you have lost all recollection of it, remember . . . You say there are no words to describe that time, you say it does not exist. But remember. Make an effort to remember. Or, failing that, invent."

Thus, we write our own liturgy, some borrowed from tradition, much of it directly from the heart. Since we are speaking of That-Which-Cannot-Be-Told, unbounded by definition, we use the metaphor of poetry. The poetry itself casts a spell. We may quote from the great woman poets, chant, or just let the sound of life flow through us: "Aaahhh . . . . " Jive talk is fine, for jive pulses the rhythm of life. Just take a deep breath, wave good-bye to your ego, and the Mother will speak through you for the goodness of all. There are no mistakes; "being in line" is not the idea. Being in laughter certainly is; she who laughs at herself and the game is three times whole.

A ritual "works" whenever spirituality is present, and spirituality is for some simply communicating with the spirits around us.

166

Others say a spiritual moment occurs whenever you sensuously and intellectually *experience* several aspects of reality as fused, aspects you usually fragment. Women's spirituality does not transcend ordinary life, but it receives power from it. Women's spirituality is not to tame the ego, but to integrate the ego with the collective self and kindred earth. Some rituals are more powerful than others, more "charged" with excitement. We feel changed. Note that these rituals are usually quite well planned, yet allow each woman to share something of herself like an act, a feeling, an experience, a ritual object.

Rituals work when magic is afoot. Vaudeville magic, or material machinations (sawing off ladies' heads?), is not the marvelous magic of the spirit. This is not to say ritual does not invigorate the material plane, but it can do far more. The great occultist and writer of another generation, Dion Fortune, defined magic as "the art of changing consciousness at will." A gift given the human species is that we can reform our whole world view, and with it our behavior. Our central nervous system can be extensively reprinted: closeted, fearful Lesbian today; proud, joyous Lesbian tomorrow. Magic? What seen and unseen forces marshaled the change? The celebration and beauty of a women's music festival? The heroism and pageantry of a Gay March on Washington? The welcoming and naming of a child parented by two women? The women who play these stories simply "make them up," mirrors for the deep magic of self-knowledge and acceptance. Such shared magic has its way with us. We "wake up" with faerie dust between our toes.

On a great, getting-up morning, celebrants often prepare for a ritual by lightly fasting or meditating. It is also important to approach a ritual in an "open" state. If you set preconditions, you are already full, full of yourself. There is little room for the living force of the ritual to flow in. Movement is another key to great ritual. "Play the Body, Free the Soul." Just breathing together can make our lungs feel like wings. We feel the Breath inside the breath. Join hands and breathe into each other's fingertips, toes, and earlobes.

Some women wonder what to wear to their first large Lesbian ritual. Open that closet door wide. Lady Clitoressa always says, "When in doubt, keep up appearances." Flash and filigree do brighten things up considerably. You can be Dame Edith Sitwell, as absolutely stylized as it is possible to be, or just wear something very precious to you. Jewelry tends to be "statement," huge rings, wide bracelets, beads and amulets. You may want to be a divine Painted Lady, with iridescent lipstick and dazzling finger lacquer. You may want to go *naturel*, clothing handwoven, colors of the earth, ornaments of the land. We don't see many women wearing petroleum products like dacron or dynel or with the M.B.A Commando look, but if you want to wear a suit and a tie to a faerie gathering, that's your business. Remember, life is a costume ball, and ritual is life quintessential.

The five Lesbian rituals which close this book are offered to inspire your own. In order to explain and not to repeat familiar womanspirit ritual conventions, here is a common format to play with. You add the imagination and daring:

1) SET UP AN ALTAR on a table or in an open cupboard, on a flat mossy rock in the woods, or in a special garden setting. Rituals are moveable feasts. It is customary for the altar to hold representations from the four elements of earth, air, fire and water, like flowers and greenery, incense, candles, a chalice or bowl of water/wine.

Most ritual objects come from earth's marketplace, but Buddhist organizations have wonderful mail order catalogs of musical instruments, statues, incense, and other ritual objects.*

2) WELCOME the celebrants and explain the ritual focus; loosely outline the sequence if necessary.

3) PURIFY THE SPACE with water or salt. CONSECRATE IT with fire and air.

4) GROUND AND CENTER THE ENERGY in order to drop away the "chatterbox" world. Celebrants can meditate on our connection with the earth, hold hands and breathe together. Be aware of "ritual bearing," hands, spine, head.

5) CAST THE SACRED CIRCLE to hold the power in, to "spirit" the space beyond the patriarchy. You can measure the circle by holding hands and mark it if you wish by corn meal, grain, red brick dust, or stones — even with a chant or song. The circle is our ring of connection. Where fathers draw lines, the Mother draws a circle. We want to face each other, not a platform or chancel, because in seeing each other, we see the Goddess. We feel part of yet another living mandala, Spirit at its core.

6) CALL IN THE FOUR DIRECTIONS to establish a firm base and orientation. "Hail, Radiant Ones!" One woman calls in each power. "Hail, Guardians of the Watchtowers of the North, power of earth and our body, the ability to listen to each living story . . . " Here improvisations can roll. The Watchtower of the East

---

* Write Dharma Crafts, 199 Auburn St., Cambridge, MA 02139, and Shasta Abbey, presided over by a woman teacher, Box 199, Mount Shasta, CA 96067. A marvelous women's "spiritual supermarket" is the Gaia Catalog Co. of *WomanSpirit Source Book* fame. Send $3 for the catalog to 1400 Shattuck Avenue, Berkeley, CA 94709.

corresponds to the element air, the energy of breath and the ability to know. The South is fire and the energy of light, the gift of spirit. The West is water, the energy of emotion and the power to dare.

7) RAISE THE ENERGY higher with movement, with music; create an altar if one is not fully set, or invoke special aspects of the Goddess.

8) DIRECT THE RAISED ENERGY to whatever main focus or activity the rite may have.

9) Be sure to "EARTH" THE POWER AND EMOTION after the ceremony is enacted to avoid feeling spaced-out, high or speedy when you must "re-enter" the plains of patriarchy. You can kneel on the earth with opened palms or share visions, ideas, feelings.

10) OPEN THE CIRCLE WITH THANKS to all, thanks for our largesse, thanks to the Goddess.

11) SHARE FOOD AND DRINK.

12) "Ritual may be formal or informal; scripted or spontaneous; structured or loose — as long as it is alive. As long as it sings." These are the words of the great Witch, Starhawk, now so powerful that the Pope in faraway Rome ordered her boss to "fire" her from her university job. She teaches on.

A Coming-Out to Mom Ritual

Despite fears of rejection and abandonment, it finally becomes too hard *not* to show and tell our family of origin or beloved friends that we are Lesbian. It is not necessary to reveal every single feeling and aspect of "the life"; this is not a confession. We, however, need to be open with loved ones, open as the normal person we are. "Passing," *in cognito, in closito* are a form of *self*-denial, and your self is too precious. Each woman tells her truth in her own time and in her own way. There is but one implacable rule of coming out: speak for yourself only; honor confidentiality. Never usurp another's right to speak out, to use her power of identity to grow. The challenge of coming out, of course, never ends (new job, new neighbors, new events), but it is also axiomatic: the more you come out, the more you can. Working out such a practice of self-accepting honesty is the key to many aspects of the good life. We Lesbians are not mainstream. In a sense, we were born with a silver spoon in our mouths. It is engraved, "self-directed," not "other-directed." Eat.

It is rarely necessary to belabor the simple, wholesome fact of gayness with casual acquaintances, any more than they would tell you the contents of their dreams and nightlife. The simplest thing to do is to assume they know — or should know — that you are a Lesbian. Take the "of course I'm gay, I wonder why everyone else isn't" attitude. People are then likely to take you at your own evaluation, concluding your self-respect and good cheer are justified. What people do not like or understand is their problem to work out. Give up any need to take on their difficulties. Ninety-nine percent of them have no power over you. Just tolerate them; many are enjoyable. There is not a super-customized, only gay way to organize a street tree-planting party, go cross-country skiing, listen to a concert, or help each other work out problems of aged parent or child care. Save your homophobia healing powers for your loved ones, for that other tiny percent who may affect bread and butter issues — and, most importantly, for yourself.

This was a ritual to support Harmony's coming-out to someone deeply important to her, a Jehovah's Witness anti-choice activist, her mother.

The space is purified and consecrated. The circle is cast, marked with rainbow glitter, the energy grounded. At the center of the altar is a large, clear glass tumbler of honey, "fixed" with spices: stick cinnamon; whole nutmegs, allspices and cloves; a piece of ginger root. A white vigil light burns behind the golden honey chalice. An old-fashioned closet (skeleton) key is placed near the glowing chalice, along with a pink paper triangle, a satin Purple Heart, and the little bottle of glitter.

The energy is raised by the women calling out in turn names of our dazzling Lesbian foremothers:

"We call on the spirit of the Moon Goddess, Diana, and her merry band of women."

"We call upon the spirits of the Amazon Warriors as well as the Convent Sisters."

"We call on Joan of Arc, the daring pirates Anne Bonny and Mary Read."

"We call on Queen Christina."

"We call on Karen Silkwood."

"We call Jane Addams, Eleanor Roosevelt, Barbara Deming, Margaret Mead."

"We call Sappho, Madame de Staël, Emily Dickinson, Willa Cather."

"We call Rosa Bonheur, Marie Laurencin, Harriet Hosmer."

"We call Gladys Bentley, Josephine Baker and Janis."

"We call Virginia Woolf and Colette."

"We call in the love of [names of current Lesbian friends/guides/lovers/heroes]."

Harmony's lover speaks. "We taste and receive the love radiance of all the Spice Women." She takes a drop of honey on her finger from the chalice, and offers it to Harmony's lips, which she then kisses.

Harmony takes the key from the altar and holds it. She tells her circle of sisters:

"In my heart, I find the GIFT OF LOVE, and it is love's nature to sing of love."

"In my heart, I find the LIGHT OF HONESTY, the power to awaken and cast away delusion. I AM LESBIAN, CHILD BELONGING TO THE UNIVERSE."

All repeat: "I AM LESBIAN, CHILD BELONGING TO THE UNIVERSE."

"In my heart, I find PATIENCE. May my mother broaden her own path to self-knowledge with my declaration of love and honesty. May I wave to her. May I be patient for at least a year and a day that our paths will meet."

"In my heart, I find DOUBT. Doubt is not the opposite of faith. It is one of the elements of faith."

All repeat: "I AM LESBIAN, CHILD OF THE UNIVERSE."

"In my heart, I find RELEASE. The energy I once spent protecting myself, like the coin of blackmail, gave me no peace. This energy is now free to nourish me."

"In my heart, I see the PINK TRIANGLE which marked my people, the gays, in Nazi concentration camps. Every time I come out, every time I honor my sisters' and brothers' right to love, I shape a different destiny. I put a circle of safety around the triangle." She draws a circle in glitter around the triangle on the altar.

All repeat: "I AM LESBIAN, CHILD BELONGING TO THE UNIVERSE."

"In my heart, I feel the beginning of a QUEST. There are monsters who would terrify me, there are Mothers who would heal me. Whatever the course, I vow to take the path with heart, lead me where it will."

All repeat: "I AM LESBIAN, CHILD OF THE UNIVERSE."

Harmony passes the key around the circle. Each woman holds it, saying, "YOU ARE A LOVER, BELOVED OF THE UNIVERSE." Anyone who wishes to offers counsel, a story of something gained in coming out publicly, or how she first had the courage to court a lover.

Harmony slowly tears the pink triangle into tiny pieces, adds glitter and tosses a handful over the circle of women. She pins on the royal purple heart, which she will keep as a charm while talking with her mother and then give to her no matter what happens.

The women close by playing Sweet Honey in the Rock's song:

Every woman who ever loved a woman
You oughta stand up and call her name
Mama — sister — daughter — lover
Every woman who ever loved a woman
You oughta stand up and call her name.

Then they break into Holly Near's "I ain't gonna get down off this riverboat," singing "honeyboat," as castanets fly. The power earthed, they dine on honeycakes and lemon tea with many a "Here I come, ready or not" and "blessed be."

A Circle of Commitment Ritual

Of the several paths to self-knowledge, the path of relationships is the socially demanding one. So, Lesbian Spirit Warrior, if you are going to "go all the way" with relationship yoga, obtain some kind of formal, social blessing as part of your medicine power. The het world tries every trick to brand a woman-loving-woman as *single*, and, most importantly, to imprint *single* into your consciousness. So, create a couple ritual however possible, even with one well-wisher or the redwoods or the animal friends as witnesses. Fully acknowledge that you are committing to a shared path. You are undergoing a rite of passage when you move in together, decide to parent a child, or pledge monogamy. Lesbians can reclaim the word "marriage" ("holy wedlock" is past saving), or use "commitment," pledge of "troth" (troth means truth), or "housewarming." We can be married under the stars, on a ferry, in the city rose garden. One of the longest-lasting marriages in Lady Clitoressa's Circle was a carefully planned ceremony which took place in the breathtaking two-minute ride up the jeweled San Francisco skyline in the Fairmont Hotel's view elevator. "She always swept me off my feet."

Consider that no woman ever faced that sexist monstrosity, a relationship "license," until 1753 in England. You may want to get in

172

bed with the state for certain of the rights and privileges which "licensees" have, or you may believe in abolishing all currently codified marriage law in favor of private contracts; that is not the point here. Do not deprive yourself of the roots, joy, clarity, and spiritual awareness which a ritual of commitment provides. Do not hold back because of some fantastical, merciless "together forever" standard. "The commitment ceremony," says Lady Clitoressa, "is useful to help us to stay awhile in order to find out what we are staying for."

Concha and Indara said they learned almost as much in planning their "circle of commitment" as they had in two years of being together. "It was an act of creation." Some friends were skittish about coming to a "wedding," so the invitations were to a "celebration of love and joyous friendship," with a "ceremony" to be held. "I asked the wary ones if all my family and friends would turn out for my funeral, why they couldn't come to my wedding," said Concha. "Our gay male friends were so supportive, some offered to be bridesmaids." It actually took a mediator to persuade certain members of the biological families to attend. Some never did, but that's show biz. Here is what they missed.

The ceremony is outdoors in a national park, next to a rushing stream. There are two altars, one to the Goddess, set with the four elements, including a huge pillar candle and a decorated apple tree to be planted later in the celebrants' garden. A Malvina Reynolds song beside it reads, "If you love, love, love me, plant a rose for me./If you think you're going to love me for a long, long time, plant an apple tree." All around the tree, there are sachets of birdseed to be tossed at the celebrants. A smaller Wedding Altar holds a "relationship candle," with "C & I" written in it and a kaleidoscopic "Earth Tray" of roots (radishes), stems (asparagus), leaves (parsley), flowers and fruit (nasturtiums and almonds). There is a bowl of pure spring water, five other tapers, two goblets of wine, and two silver needles. There is a scroll. The celebrants each carry bouquets to exchange and place on the Goddess Altar. As they stand, a lavender blue cape flows in the wind, an iridescent scarf. A flute plays. They each wear a rainbow cord around one ankle to show that, as of today, they are neither bound, nor free.

High Priestess: All Welcome! We come to witness and celebrate the decision of Concha and Indara to share their lives. We want to help them do so! Though I am a Priestess of the Goddess, no religion requires an agent to marry a couple. Judaism prescribes only two witnesses be present from the tribe; in their absence, Heaven and Earth may serve. In marrying themselves, Indara and Concha become ministers to one another, knowing their own inner universe, their own minds, hearts and bodies are their church. Will you all clasp hands for a few moments to affirm Concha and Indara's commitment?

Indara's "Best Woman": You, Indara and Concha, stand in the charmed circle of your love, as it should be. But love was not meant to be possessed by two women alone. At the end of your days, may you be able to say, "Because you have loved me, because I have loved you, I have loved the whole world."

Concha's "Best Woman": In the words of George Sand, great woman writer and beacon of free love, "Let us remain altogether young and trembling right into old age, and let us try to fancy that we are merely starting out our life right up to the very eve of death . . . I am an optimist in spite of everything that has torn me to shreds; it is perhaps my only quality."

High Priestess to Relatives: Will you as parents [sisters, brothers, children] rise to give Concha and Indara your blessings and pledge to them your love and acceptance?

Relatives: [Rising.] We do.

The Eternal Flame

Indara and Concha each take a candle from the Wedding Altar and light it from the Goddess Altar candle. They then light their relationship candle together. This candle is to be saved and lit each season, or when they have a large decision to make, or when they have a serious argument.

The Bond

Concha and Indara prick their fingers with the silver needles which are first passed through fire, then water. They let the blood flow into the bowl of spring water. Each pours a bit of this rosé into one another's goblet of wine. They pour a libation to the earth, toast and drink, saying, "May you never thirst." They feed one another from the Earth Tray, saying, "May you never hunger."

The Vows

High Priestess: What vows do you bring to this occasion? [Indara and Concha take the scroll from the altar and alternately read.]

Concha: We take the vow of fidelity, which to us means to speak the truth with love, to share life openly, to stay close to reality.

Indara: We take the vow of risk, to be vulnerable to a love that risks what we are for the sake of what we can become.

Concha: We vow to talk, even when it is easier not to, to keep sending messages, to listen, knowing we are committed to the path, even when we do not know the way.

Indara: We vow to walk in empathy and compassion.

Concha: We vow to try together, to pledge this as a year of union, one ever renewable, season after season.

Indara: We vow to grow together always, honoring our history, no matter what form our relationship takes.

Concha: We vow to release the need to manufacture hardship, to create dark drama.

Indara: We vow to be happy, not to forget who we are and who we want to be.

Concha: We vow to laugh in joy and in our folly.

Indara: We vow to celebrate our sensuality.

Concha: We vow not only to share our joys and successes, but to accept each other's mood swings, sorrows and failures.

Indara: In this, we vow to love the Sun which feeds us, the Sun which also throws our shadows.

Concha: We vow to appoint one another the guardian and greeter of each other's times of solitude.

Indara: We vow to let that which is different between us exist and be itself.

High Priestess: With these vows, may you trust one another, trust life and not be afraid. Remember to be one another's best friend. [All three light a candle from the relationship candle and place them on the Goddess Altar.]

The Ring Ceremony

High Priestess: What pledge do you offer in exchange of these vows?

Indara: I offer this ring, ancient woman circle, most perfect of forms.

Concha: And I offer this ring, an outward symbol of our inner commitment.

High Priestess: Indara, as you place this ring on Concha's finger, please repeat, "This is my beloved, this is my best friend."

Indara: This is my beloved, this is my best friend.

High Priestess: Concha, as you place this ring on Indara's finger, please repeat, "This is my beloved, this is my best friend.""

Concha: This is my beloved, this is my best friend.

[All sigh.]

Publication of Vows

High Priestess: In making public this bond of unity, Indara and Concha hereby plight their "troth," their truth. Let all honor their decision and the threshold of their home. Amidst conflict, may Concha and Indara remember this day of affirmation and serenity; in the twilight of despair, remember the courage and hope of this ceremony shared with your loved ones.

Indara's Best Woman: Now let us celebrate this loving union! Let us kiss the brides and dance and sing!

Concha's Best Woman: Please water the little apple tree with your good wishes, and take a sachet of birdseed to throw when Indara and Concha leave for their honeymoon.

The music begins to play, the bubbles float, the rainbow flag is raised, and the Goddess claps her hands.

A Midsummer Dyke's Dream

The invitation reads: *Come celebrate the Month-of-Yes-You-May! Winter is banished. The lap of the Goddess is filling with flowers as sweet desire weds wild delight! Let us quicken to Earth's songs of union and dance with Her in ecstasy, peace and love. Women's Mysteries are afoot in the fires of Beltane. Couples, fan your flames! Singles, inflame your fans!*

The Queen of the May will provide childcare for shame, guilt, pain and jealousy this one night of the year. Bring sleeping bags. Dress optional.

The ritual is to be celebrated at a beautiful home on five private acres of woodland. Sixteen Lesbians are invited who are aware of, or initiated in, the ancient, sacred Women's Mystery Celebrations. These were sensual/spiritual ceremonies to the Goddess performed in secret by women only at the temple of the Earth Mother Demeter in Eleusis before the patriarchal conquest of Greece. On some level, all women hold the Mystery prayers in their wombs. Suffice it to say (although every true Mystery is beyond words), that the Mysteries evoke the swirling powers of life, death and rebirth, and they embrace sexual fires of transformation in their multi-layered, most universal and deepest essence. Such energy was and is the quintessential threat to the patriarchy's need to profane women's divine, and temporal, powers; to the masculinist denial of all deep feelings from ecstasy to grief; and to the warrior's battle to control, even sterilize, nature. The tide is turning, but until the life-force is ascendant in humans again, celebrate the Mysteries in glowing secrecy.

Remember, too, that flowering womanhood is especially powerful in group focus, so individual erotophobia will struggle harder to distort reality. The word "taboo" once meant "sacred"; most sensual taboos of today were especially sanctioned by or beloved of the Goddess. All this ritual joy is so new (again) that we need to be as careful and gentle with one another as we would be with a round-eyed newborn. For example, in celebrating the Mysteries this May eve we reserved special places for ceremonial "alone times." Two seasoned priestesses of Aphrodite offered to take turns as listening counselors if anyone wanted to "check in" big emotions.

Cautionary notes out of the way, let us go a'Maying, happy that all the earth religions consider pleasure a virtue. The Goddess of the Old Religion smiles, "All acts of love and pleasure are my rituals," and says, "Celebrate yourself and you will see the self is everywhere."

Three great bonfires burn in the soft dusk. A garlanded sign on the path to the lawn reads, "You are entering the Temple of the Queen of the May, where shame is unknown and unnecessary."

As we arrive, everyone is asked to visit the triptych-like decorated shower next to the hot tub, to ritually bathe and become "sky clad" if we wish. A full-length, candle-lit mirror stands beside the shower, where a tape sings the slow, wondrous chant, "This is MY body, and I LIKE HER." A large bowl of salt water stands to receive and purify any prejudices one may hold tonight against her beautiful body. A nearby tree is hung with eight emerald green and eight royal blue ribbons. Couples don contrasting colors. Around the tree are sixteen tiny May baskets of meadowsweet seeds to plant in the woods. A banner in the tree says, "The Goddess is looking through your eyes. Are you showing Her a good time?"

When all gather on the lawn, the space is purified and consecrated. The circle is cast with perfumed water, and is closed; the Goddess protects Her celebrants. Demeter's altar stands to the north, banked with thirteen kinds of flowers. A ceramic chalice of deep rose holds aphrodisiacs of ginseng, cannabis and ravishing spices. Since Demeter is the "natural woman," there is nothing processed on Her altar. She is offered honeycomb, unpressed grapes, uncooked grain, and unspun wool; no honeycakes, wine or cloth. The mystical, dildoesque fetish of the Mysteries, "an ear of corn reaped in silence," is present in colorful Indian corn.

In the center of the circle is a huge cauldron, bordered with ivy and soft fennel plumes. A fire is lit in it, and a libation is made to the earth. Each woman touches the tips of her fingers and the tips of her thumbs together pointing downward in the sensuous symbol of Demeter, Whose name means "Mother of the Delta." The women breathe together and relax, one breath, one organism.

The women begin to channel the Goddess of Ten Thousand Names as they are moved to invoke Her names:

"Hail Radiant Ones!"

"Hail Demeter, Durga, Istar & Isis, Earth Mothers and Mistresses of Mysteries."

"Hail Diana, Weaver of Enchantments. A welcome to Your love tribe of moonwomen."

"Hail Maenads and Bacchantes swept into ecstasy."

"Hail Voodoo Queens, dancing your power and pleasure in Congo Square."

"Hail Baubo of Eleusis, Goddess of the Belly Laugh, Who raised Her Skirt and danced to cheer the Earth Mother, lonely for Her daughter."

"Hail Uzume, Japanese Goddess of Merriment, Who danced so erotically, in such ribald humor, She charmed the Sun Goddess, Amaterasu, to return."

"Hail Cybele, Great Mother of the Ancient Near East, a welcome to Your votaries and the Corybantes, who dance to cymbal and drum."

"Hail Brigid, Celtic Triple Goddess, Guardian of the Beltane Fires and Maypole. Welcome to Your great Priestess of Avalon, Morgan Le Fay."

"Hail Kali, Queen of the Tantric-Ringed Embrace."

"Hail Venus Aphrodite, and Your poet-priestess Sappho. Hail, African Oshun, Goddess of Love."

"Blessed are You, Source of the Universe.
Feed us on warm flowers with wide open mouths.
Honor All, Goddess Within All."

Each woman in turn anoints her neighbor in the circle with lavender-scented oil. "I purify you of shame and anxiety. I anoint you with the joyous Life Force."

The women lie down in a great mandala wheel, feet toward the warm cauldron, couples side by side, green and blue ribbons alternating around the circle. A little tricky, but we figure it out in laughter. The beat of drums takes up residence in our blood.

High Priestess: "We come together to kindle the Radiant Core. If you have never done this before in a group, the Greater Mandala, this is the time. Sacred ritual forms make it safe and pleasurable. Blue be-ribboned women, your communion at the bells is to *give* the Five-Fold Kiss of the Goddess to your nearby goddess in green ribbon. At the next chimes, lie back and pause, no matter how tempting to go on. With the sound of more chiming, *receive* the Five-Fold Kiss from your goddess in green. Then repeat the same with the goddess on your opposite side. Our supplies of kisses are infinite.

"Stay centered in your heart and belly, connected with Heaven and Earth, powerful and relaxed. At times you will feel energy extroverted and assertive, at times subtle and inward."

[The Five-Fold Kiss of the Goddess is to kiss a woman five times in five special places: first on the forehead and eyes; next on the lips; then her breasts; her vulva; finally her feet. "Tongue gloves" (dental dams) are of course available.]

Two Priestesses sing alternately, ringing gold chimes:
"Embrace the earth-green woman, sky-blue lady."
"As you temple-kiss, celebrate the Goddess."
"Breast-kiss, to nurture you in love."
"Now a Yoni kiss, to merge with the Great All."
"Kiss the feet, for touching the Earth and bringing you to this circle."

[Repeat three more cycles of sky and earth-ribboned women kissing.]

After this sweet grazing, the women slowly rise and begin to circle dance, spinning faster and faster. Couples leap over the cauldron of fire to burn away their petty disagreements and to rekindle sensuous fires. We dally forth to feast and bring in the May . . .

At dawn, we gather to let even Aphrodesia go, in Her manner of ebb and flow. We deeply thank the Queen of the May and her priestesses. The circle is open, but unbroken, a bond blooming in the May.

Breaking Up,
a Transformation Ritual

This is a ritual to mark the evolution of a lover into a primary, for-life-friend, to mark the something-lost, something-gained in all change. A continuing strong connection is of course not always

179

possible or even wise, and must be a deeply considered mutual decision. Such a bridging ceremony usually doesn't work if it is attempted before physical withdrawal or before major grievances receive some kind of closure. Focus is blessedly on the n-o-w, with all rehash behind. At last, memory has collected its ransom and taken pity. The reasons for a break-up are ultimately not as interesting as how you handle them. There is never anything wrong in love; she just happens. In the end, it only matters where she takes you.

The "break-up" is really of the struggle. The massive struggle of relating as primary lovers, this emotional dam of tight weirs woven across a once open vision, has finally loosened. You have let go of the intensity of the struggle, and have let the dam break, the most merciful thing you could do for each other. You know love energy has a chance to flow again, but only if you can ride what Lady Clitoressa calls the "One-Step Program" of the two waves: Love and Let Go Love and Let Go Love and Let Go . . . . This demands only the valor of living your own ego death and the daring to release your pain and grief. Drop the shroud of pain and you have nothing to protect yourself from being composted back into rebirth. But whoever said that being born was easy? If you make it, do call a ritual to celebrate and nourish the transformation.

This is a far from compensatory rite. It may be more meaningful and lasting than a "Circle of Commitment" ritual because you have already met the power struggle by going far into yourselves. You know the dark passage. You may now emerge together into a new kind of commitment and co-creation. Disruption is the great awakener. As May Sarton wrote at fifty-eight: "I have only begun to understand what love is . . . forced to my knees again and again like a gardener planting seeds and weeding, so that I may once more bring a relationship to flower, keep it truly alive." Relationships are endings and beginnings with emptiness, newness and germination in between.

Because they envisioned relationship as spiraling into friendship, Billie and Aurelia returned to the same park in the wine country where they had pledged their troth four years before. As the "art to part" would have it, now it was winter; then it was blazing summer. Now the leaves along the path to the stream were laced with ice, the trees stark and glistening. They were again under a new moon and brilliant sunlight. "We almost frolicked along the path, touching each other, yet often silent. In some ways the earth was even more beautiful than long ago. More seasoned? As we neared the stream we began humming, then singing the old chant:

Everything She touches changes.
She changes everything She touches.

"We helped one another over the rushing stream and saw a place for an altar on the steep bank. Over the roots of one tree was a great lap of moss. In its center we placed a Y-shaped lichened branch to show 'the road to heaven sometimes forks' and two bright yellow margarita flowers from the hotel garden. We had also brought a red vigil light, incense, two bowls, an egg, some cranberries and bee pollen, and a bag of 'magic mix.' The beautiful mix was a wealth of beans of all colors, sweet herbs, vegetable and flower seeds, grains and whole spices. We blew our warm breath over it and kissed."

Billie: "As the candle melts, our struggles melt."

Aurelia, lighting the candle: "Blessed is the match consumed in kindling the flame."

Billie: "A flame the same and different."

Aurelia: "Blessed is the flame that burns in the special places of the heart."

Each fills her bowl with water from "the stream of forgiveness" and returns to the altar.

Both say: "We are a part of the Body of Women."

Aurelia and Billie say alternately: "If I have hurt you, forgive me."

Each says what she forgives, then pours her water, "water which bears no wound," onto the earth.

Aurelia and Billie say alternately: "If I have touched you, return the touch."

Each tells the blessings the relationship has brought her and touches the face of the other.

Aurelia and Billie say alternately: "If I need you, I too will be here for you."

Each tells what she needs from the other now as a heart-friend. They each pour the "magic mix of blessings and responsibilities" into one another's bowl and scatter a handful over the earth.

Aurelia and Billie say alternately: "What do we lose to the Dark Goddess of Change?"

Each tells her own hardship at not being love partners and is fed the sharp bitterness of the cranberry.

Aurelia and Billie say alternately: "What do we renew by the Dark Goddess of Change?"

181

Each tells what she wishes to plant in the friendship and is fed the rich sweetness of bee pollen.

Billie cracks the egg before the candle, setting the two shells beside it on the moss. She says, "This relationship has birthed and nourished treasures for both of us. We now set it free to go out into the world to share its gifts." Aurelia pours red wax from the candle onto the white shells.

Aurelia and Billie each write three hopes on a separate piece of paper, send them down the stream and tell each other these dreams. Four years ago, they had privately buried their fears in the soil. *Aurelia and Billie hold hands and say:*

> *O Mother, rejoice with us,*
> *The circle is open, but unbroken.*
> *May the peace of the Goddess remain in our hearts.*
> *Merry meet. Merry part.*
> *And merry meet again.*

They each take magic mix home to put in a glass jar in the sun. They kiss, hug, cry, and kiss again in reunion.

A Lesbian Self-Blessing Ritual

You are your own best lover. Life herself is your sweetheart. What a tandem. But how rarely we tap into the redolent power and profundity of our own body making love with its universe. We so often major in the entirely different energy of social forces. Sometimes when you play with your own goddess, why not make a production of it? Treat her like your wisest and most sensitive lover is coming home. This can be quite social in its own way. You may have a whole cast of characters to calm down with foreplay: the creator, the parent, the child, the woman, the man, the warrior, the energy exporter, the accountant, the judge, the trouble shooter. The trouble shooter, for example, works gruelling overtime and especially needs to rest. You don't keep slaves, do you?

Let's take everyone to the theater, one presented by special attunement to reveal dramas of meaning, well-being and ecstasy. Admission: free, with no new complications. Time: the powerful waxing or full moon. Sets: a bedroom and a bathtub. Flowers you arrange for yourself. A candle which you have slowly rubbed with your favorite scented oil and inscribed with your self-anointed name. A chalice, which typically symbolizes pleasure and will also be holding power. A red pen that runs like hot blood, and little slips of paper. A natural object to be a metaphor for you of the Creatrix. I often use a chambered nautilus sea shell. In order to float, the magical creature who lived there continuously creates a spiral of pearled chambers built one onto the other. It lives only in the roomiest and most open one. I also place a power object on the altar to be "re-charged," like my flat, pocket-sized driftwood piece, licked almost to satin by the ocean and now polished by my thigh and fingers. Let a dish of salt sit by to absorb any negative guests at the party. Chimes or bells or a Tibetan singing bowl can be present to wake up your lover and enfold her in a chord of sound. Pleasure tools may also be placed on the altar to be recharged. A ribbon of rice, whole cloves and saffron can secure your space inside the threshold of the closed bedroom door.

Every powerful, romantic quest is, of course, a treat in brilliant improvisation, but here is one "Theater of the Self" in five acts.

Purify

I take an exquisitely long bath or shower, enacting something like the sweat lodge ritual. First, I wash away the angers and grudges, spitting water from my lips. I carefully rub fear from every crevice. There is no point in doing a nude ritual if I'm clothed with old burdens. I watch the angers and fears swirl down the drain. Cleansed, I let the water flow all over me, taking the form of my visions. I ask assistance in creating these hopes, feeling generous energy waves flowing around me. In gratitude, I carefully dry and cream every inch of this marvelous animal who always accompanies me to the Theater.

Relax and Center

I lie down in my room like I'm on a warm, soft, grassy plain. All my hairs, even the downy ones on my neck, are roots exchanging nurturance with the earth. I tense, then relax every muscle; I breathe slowly into every body part, sweeping tension away. I can pause between each breath to feel my body and the earth.

My mind wants to empty, to rest at last from its eternal commentary on the daily stimulus hurricane. So I focus only on the nautilus' grace, the flowers, the candle flame. I can count my breaths, to ten and backwards, the tiniest units of concentration, which provide a haven from invading baroque fantasies. Whenever chatter floats in, I just wave and go back to the count. To negative squalls, I say, "Go in peace," and nod toward the sparkling salt.

When I am relaxed, feeling calm and at ease, I can look at any fears and griefs which are coming up. I try to think of each anxiety as a beam of light aimed to show me something, while recognizing it selects and edits realities. I write down each "negative" as a label on one side of a slip of paper. On the other side, I write a word for the same feeling's possible light or wisdom. Sometimes I can barely guess a benefit, perhaps only a "go slow," or "let go." I put the worry/wisdom under the chalice. At last, with fanfare of music, I write the word "COURAGE" in bold red caps. I kiss this paper with "COURAGE" and swirl it around the chalice of water. It flows in carmine streams, penetrating all the space it is given.

Chalice of Protection

I bow to the altar and say aloud, "Bless me, Mother, for I am Your child." I dip two fingers in the chalice and touch these parts of my nude body, saying:

"I anoint my temples. Bless this mind to weave in beauty."

"I anoint my eyes. Bless these eyes to see clearly."

"I anoint my nose. Bless this nose to breathe deeply."

"I anoint my lips. Bless this mouth to speak truth."

"I anoint my ears. Bless these ears to hear truth."

"I anoint my breasts. Bless these breasts to nourish me in strength."

"I anoint my heart. Bless this heart to fill with love."

"I anoint my womb. Bless this womb to serve the life force."

"I anoint my feet. Bless these feet to know the path."

Chalice of Pleasure

I ring the chimes. I dip each finger of one hand into the chalice, then press them to the other hand's fingertips. I bow to the altar. I say, "I anoint my fingers. Bless these hands to create pleasure."

I take a piece of amber, the fragrant resin from India, press it in my left palm and draw a rich line with it up my arm, over to my heart and down to my curly hairline. I oil my hands, inhale my body. I caress my skin all over, loving its textures from foot soles to inner thigh, to lips, ears and eyelids. I sing that my lover is returning. I squeeze the corridors of my womb and gateless gate, winking at my love, my love who will do anything to please me. Circling, squeezing, sliding the glistening hood of my clitoris back and forth, I feel a dewy moonrose opening. As I begin to feel like one heartbeat all over, I open myself fully, and then pause. I pause to look, look deep and long, as if exploring a flower in heady bloom. I see the clitoris, this one organ of the body created for pleasure and pleasure alone,

184

swollen with the plentitude of it all. And she takes me in every way, my hips, even my fingertips flowering . . . across the Great Divide.

Earth the Power
I stretch, luxuriate, let my toes curl. I feel pregnant with a new self. I stay with the good feelings of any and all plateaus: peace, sensuality, orgasm, affection, tenderness. I can come back any time to my divine companion. Goddess, do love my Whoopee.

Goddess,

Do Love My Whoopee.

Index

187

Books from Cleis Press

REFERENCE

Putting Out: The Essential Publishing Resource Guide For Lesbian and Gay Writers
by Edisol W. Dotson.
ISBN: 0-939416-86-7 29.95 cloth;
ISBN: 0-939416-87-5 12.95 paper.

LESBIAN STUDIES

Boomer: Railroad Memoirs
by Linda Niemann.
ISBN: 0-939416-55-7 12.95 paper.

The Case of the Good-For-Nothing Girlfriend
by Mabel Maney.
ISBN: 0-939416-90-5 24.95 cloth;
ISBN: 0-939416-91-3 10.95 paper.

The Case of the Not-So-Nice Nurse
by Mabel Maney.
ISBN: 0-939416-75-1 24.95 cloth;
ISBN: 0-939416-76-X 9.95 paper.

Dagger: On Butch Women
edited by Roxxie, Lily Burana, Linnea Due.
ISBN: 0-939416-81-6 29.95 cloth;
ISBN: 0-939416-82-4 14.95 paper.

Daughters of Darkness: Lesbian Vampire Stories
edited by Pam Keesey.
ISBN: 0-939416-77-8 24.95 cloth;
ISBN: 0-939416-78-6 9.95 paper.

Different Daughters: A Book by Mothers of Lesbians
edited by Louise Rafkin.
ISBN: 0-939416-12-3 21.95 cloth;
ISBN: 0-939416-13-1 9.95 paper.

Different Mothers: Sons & Daughters of Lesbians Talk About Their Lives
edited by Louise Rafkin.
ISBN: 0-939416-40-9 24.95 cloth;
ISBN: 0-939416-41-7 9.95 paper.

Girlfriend Number One: Lesbian Life in the '90s
edited by Robin Stevens.
ISBN: 0-939416-79-4 29.95 cloth;
ISBN: 0-939416-8 12.95 paper.

Hothead Paisan: Homicidal Lesbian Terrorist
by Diane DiMassa.
ISBN: 0-939416-73-5 14.95 paper.

A Lesbian Love Advisor
by Celeste West.
ISBN: 0-939416-27-1 24.95 cloth;
ISBN: 0-939416-26-3 9.95 paper.

Long Way Home: The Odyssey of a Lesbian Mother and Her Children
by Jeanne Jullion.
ISBN: 0-939416-05-0 8.95 paper.

More Serious Pleasure: Lesbian Erotic Stories and Poetry
edited by the Sheba Collective.
ISBN: 0-939416-48-4 24.95 cloth;
ISBN: 0-939416-47-6 9.95 paper.

The Night Audrey's Vibrator Spoke: A Stonewall Riots Collection
by Andrea Natalie.
ISBN: 0-939416-64-6 8.95 paper.

Queer and Pleasant Danger: Writing Out My Life
by Louise Rafkin.
ISBN: 0-939416-60-3 24.95 cloth;
ISBN: 0-939416-61-1 9.95 paper.

Rubyfruit Mountain: A Stonewall Riots Collection
by Andrea Natalie.
ISBN: 0-939416-74-3 9.95 paper.

Serious Pleasure: Lesbian Erotic Stories and Poetry
edited by the Sheba Collective.
ISBN: 0-939416-46-8 24.95 cloth;
ISBN: 0-939416-45-X 9.95 paper.

SEXUAL POLITICS

Good Sex: Real Stories from Real People
by Julia Hutton.
ISBN: 0-939416-56-5 24.95 cloth;
ISBN: 0-939416-57-3 12.95 paper.

The Good Vibrations Guide to Sex: How to Have Safe, Fun Sex in the '90s
by Cathy Winks and Anne Semans.
ISBN: 0-939416-83-2 29.95;
ISBN: 0-939416-84-0 14.95 paper.

Madonnarama: Essays on Sex and Popular Culture
edited by Lisa Frank and Paul Smith.
ISBN: 0-939416-72-7 24.95 cloth;
ISBN: 0-939416-71-9 9.95 paper.

Public Sex: The Culture of Radical Sex
by Pat Califia.
ISBN: 0-939416-88-3 29.95 cloth;
ISBN: 0-939416-89-1 12.95 paper.

Sex Work: Writings by Women in the Sex Industry
edited by Frédérique Delacoste and Priscilla Alexander.
ISBN: 0-939416-10-7 24.95 cloth;
ISBN: 0-939416-11-5 16.95 paper.

Susie Bright's Sexual Reality: A Virtual Sex World Reader
by Susie Bright.
ISBN: 0-939416-58-1 24.95 cloth;
ISBN: 0-939416-59-X 9.95 paper.

Susie Sexpert's Lesbian Sex World
by Susie Bright.
ISBN: 0-939416-34-4 24.95 cloth;
ISBN: 0-939416-35-2 9.95 paper.

FICTION

Another Love
by Erzsébet Galgóczi.
ISBN: 0-939416-52-2 24.95 cloth;
ISBN: 0-939416-51-4 8.95 paper.

Cosmopolis: Urban Stories by Women
edited by Ines Rieder.
ISBN: 0-939416-36-0 24.95 cloth;
ISBN: 0-939416-37-9 9.95 paper.

Dirty Weekend: A Novel of Revenge
by Helen Zahavi.
ISBN: 0-939416-85-9 10.95 paper.

A Forbidden Passion
by Cristina Peri Rossi.
ISBN: 0-939416-64-0 24.95 cloth;
ISBN: 0-939416-68-9 9.95 paper.

In the Garden of Dead Cars
by Sybil Claiborne.
ISBN: 0-939416-65-4 24.95 cloth;
ISBN: 0-939416-66-2 9.95 paper.

Night Train To Mother
by Ronit Lentin.
ISBN: 0-939416-29-8 24.95 cloth;
ISBN: 0-939416-28-X 9.95 paper.

The One You Call Sister: New Women's Fiction
edited by Paula Martinac.
ISBN: 0-939416-30-1 24.95 cloth;
ISBN: 0-939416031-X 9.95 paper.

Only Lawyers Dancing
by Jan McKemmish.
ISBN: 0-939416-70-0 24.95 cloth;
ISBN: 0-939416-69-7 9.95 paper.

Unholy Alliances: New Women's Fiction
edited by Louise Rafkin.
ISBN: 0-939416-14-X 21.95 cloth;
ISBN: 0-939416-15-8 9.95 paper.

The Wall
by Marlen Haushofer.
ISBN: 0-939416-53-0 24.95 cloth;
ISBN: 0-939416-54-9 paper.

We Came All The Way from Cuba So You Could Dress Like This?: Stories
by Achy Obejas.
ISBN: 0-939416-92-1 24.95 cloth;
ISBN: 0-939416-93-X 10.95 paper.

LATIN AMERICA

Beyond the Border: A New Age in Latin American Women's Fiction
edited by Nora Erro-Peralta and Caridad Silva-Núñez.
ISBN: 0-939416-42-5 24.95 cloth;
ISBN: 0-939416-43-3 12.95 paper.

The Little School: Tales of Disappearance and Survival in Argentina
by Alicia Partnoy.
ISBN: 0-939416-08-5 21.95 cloth;
ISBN: 0-939416-07-7 9.95 paper.

Revenge of the Apple
by Alicia Partnoy.
ISBN: 0-939416-62-X 24.95 cloth;
ISBN: 0-939416-63-8 8.95 paper.

You Can't Drown the Fire: Latin American Women Writing in Exile
edited by Alicia Partnoy.
ISBN: 0-939416-16-6 24.95 cloth;
ISBN: 0-939416-17-4 9.95 paper.

POLITICS OF HEALTH

The Absence of the Dead Is Their Way of Appearing
by Mary Winfrey Trautmann.
ISBN: 0-939416-04-2 8.95 paper.

AIDS: The Women
edited by Ines Rieder and Patricia Ruppelt.
ISBN: 0-939416-20-4 24.95 cloth;
ISBN: 0-939416-21-2 9.95 paper

Don't: A Woman's Word
by Elly Danica.
ISBN: 0-939416-23-9 21.95 cloth;
ISBN: 0-939416-22-0 8.95 paper

1 in 3: Women with Cancer Confront an Epidemic
edited by Judith Brady.
ISBN: 0-939416-50-6 24.95 cloth;
ISBN: 0-939416-49-2 10.95 paper.

Voices in the Night: Women Speaking About Incest
edited by Toni A.H. McNaron and Yarrow Morgan.
ISBN: 0-939416-02-6 9.95 paper.

With the Power of Each Breath: A Disabled Women's Anthology
edited by Susan Browne, Debra Connors and Nanci Stern.
ISBN: 0-939416-09-3 24.95 cloth;
ISBN: 0-939416-06-9 10.95 paper.

Woman-Centered Pregnancy and Birth
by the Federation of Feminist Women's Health Centers.
ISBN: 0-939416-03-4 11.95 paper.

AUTOBIOGRAPHY, BIOGRAPHY, LETTERS

Peggy Deery:
An Irish Family at War
by Nell McCafferty.
ISBN: 0-939416-38-7 24.95 cloth;
ISBN: 0-939416-39-5 9.95 paper.

The Shape of Red:
Insider/Outsider Reflections
*by Ruth Hubbard and
Margaret Randall.*
ISBN: 0-939416-19-0 24.95 cloth;
ISBN: 0-939416-18-2 9.95 paper.

Women & Honor:
Some Notes on Lying
by Adrienne Rich.
ISBN: 0-939416-44-1 3.95 paper.

ANIMAL RIGHTS

And a Deer's Ear, Eagle's Song
and Bear's Grace: Relationships
Between Animals and Women
*edited by Theresa Corrigan and
Stephanie T. Hoppe.*
ISBN: 0-939416-38-7 24.95 cloth;
ISBN: 0-939416-39-5 9.95 paper.

With a Fly's Eye, Whale's Wit and
Woman's Heart: Relationships
Between Animals and Women
*edited by Theresa Corrigan and
Stephanie T. Hoppe.*
ISBN: 0-939416-24-7 24.95 cloth;
ISBN: 0-939416-25-5 9.95 paper.

Since 1980, Cleis Press has published progressive books by women. We welcome your order and will ship your books as quickly as possible. Individual orders must be prepaid (U.S. dollars only). Please add 15% shipping. PA residents add 6% sales tax. Mail orders: Cleis Press, P.O. Box 8933, Pittsburgh PA 15221. MasterCard and Visa orders: include account number, exp. date, and signature. FAX your credit card order: (412) 937-1567. Or, phone us Mon-Fri, 9am–5pm EST: (412) 937-1555.